Tradition in Tension

Theological Perspectives from Congar and Kung

by

Dr. ant

Tradition in Tension: Theological Perspectives from Congar and Kung

Tradition in Tension: Theological Perspectives from Congar and Kung

Contents

Introduction

In the expansive and intricate landscape of Roman Catholic theology, tradition stands as a cornerstone upon which the understanding and interpretation of Sacred Scripture are built. The relationship between Scripture and tradition is both ancient and ever-evolving, presenting a dynamic interplay that speaks to the heart of the Church's mission and purpose. This book seeks to delve into the enduring significance of this relationship, tracing its development through the centuries and examining the profound ways in which tradition has shaped, and continues to shape, the faith and practice of the Roman Catholic Church.

The term "tradition" originates from the Latin word *traditio*, meaning "to hand over" or "to deliver." In the context of Roman Catholicism, tradition refers to the living transmission of the Church's teachings, life, and worship, under the guidance of the Holy Spirit. It is through this sacred deposit of faith that the Church, the Bride of Christ, continues to speak to the world, conveying the immutable and eternal truths revealed by God. Tradition is not a static relic of the past but a living and active force that shapes the present and future of the Church.

The development of Catholic theology is a testament to the enduring vitality and relevance of tradition. From the apostolic era to the present day, the Church has navigated numerous challenges and controversies, always returning to the wellspring of tradition to find answers and guidance. Throughout the centuries, theologians, scholars, and Church Fathers have contributed to the rich tapestry of tradition, each adding their voice to the ongoing conversation and deepening the Church's understanding of divine revelation.

Central to this exploration is the recognition that tradition and Sacred Scripture are not separate or competing sources of divine revelation. Rather, they are intrinsically linked, each illuminating and interpreting the other. The Second Vatican Council, in its Dogmatic Constitution on Divine Revelation, *Dei Verbum,* emphasized this point, stating that

Scripture and tradition "flow from the same divine wellspring" and "form one sacred deposit of the word of God."

As we journey through the pages of this book, we will encounter the thoughts and contributions of seminal figures in the history of Christian thought, such as Yves Congar and Hans Küng, whose work on tradition has sparked both admiration and controversy. Their perspectives provide valuable insights into the ongoing dialogue about the role of tradition in the life of the Church. Additionally, we will explore the historical milestones that have shaped the development of tradition, from the early apostolic Church and the medieval scholastics to the transformative impacts of the Reformation, Counter-Reformation, Enlightenment, and Modernity.

Through this exploration, we aim to shed light on the ways in which tradition has been understood, interpreted, and applied across different historical and cultural contexts. By examining the contributions of key theologians and the decisions of ecumenical councils, we will uncover the complexities and nuances that have characterized the development of Catholic theology. Our goal is not only to trace the historical evolution of tradition but also to consider its contemporary relevance and future trajectory in a rapidly changing world.

The role of tradition in Catholic doctrine and practice cannot be overstated. From liturgical practices and sacramental theology to the teachings of the Magisterium, tradition permeates every aspect of the Church's life. It is through tradition that the Church maintains its continuity with the apostolic faith while engaging with the challenges and opportunities of the present. In our examination of tradition, we will consider its implications for ecumenical dialogue and interfaith relations, recognizing its potential to be both a source of unity and a point of contention.

Ultimately, this book is an invitation to reflect on the profound mystery of divine revelation as conveyed through tradition and Sacred Scripture. It is an opportunity to consider how the Church, through the guidance of the Holy Spirit, continues to hand down the faith once delivered to the saints. In a world marked by rapid change and uncertainty, the enduring truths of the faith remain a steadfast beacon, offering hope and guidance to all who seek to understand the mind and heart of God.

As we embark on this journey, let us remain mindful of the words of St. Vincent of Lerins, who articulated the principles of doctrinal development in his famous *Commonitorium*: "We hold that faith which has been believed everywhere, always, by all." This timeless affirmation underscores the universality and continuity of the Catholic faith, grounded in the sacred tradition that unites believers across time and space.

With this introduction, we set the stage for a comprehensive exploration of the interplay between tradition and Sacred Scripture in Roman Catholic theology. We will trace the historical development of tradition, examining its foundations, evolution, and impact on the Church's understanding of divine revelation. Through the insights of key theologians and the decisions of ecumenical councils, we will uncover the richness and complexity of tradition as it has been handed down through the ages.

In doing so, we hope to offer a deeper appreciation of the ways in which tradition continues to shape the faith and practice of the Roman Catholic Church. By examining the theological tensions and resolutions that have emerged throughout history, we aim to provide a nuanced and comprehensive understanding of tradition's role in the life of the Church. As we look to the future, we will consider the challenges and opportunities that lie ahead, exploring the prospects for the evolution of tradition in a changing world.

In summary, this book is dedicated to illuminating the intricate tapestry of tradition and Sacred Scripture, exploring their interwoven narratives and the profound ways in which they continue to inform and inspire the Roman Catholic faith. May this journey enrich our understanding and deepen our appreciation of the timeless truths that have been handed down to us through the centuries.

Chapter 1: Understanding Tradition in Roman Catholic Theology

The essence of Roman Catholic theology is inextricably linked to the concept of Tradition, a dynamic yet immutable conduit that bridges the divine and the human. Tradition in Catholicism is not merely a collection of texts or rituals handed down through generations; it's the living transmission of the faith itself, enveloping Sacred Scripture with the richness of centuries-old practices, teachings, and communal experiences. From the apostolic era, where the first whispers of Tradition began to take shape, to its evolution through the Councils and the development of doctrinal tenets, this perennial continuum has been a beacon guiding the faithful toward an understanding of the eternal truths revealed by God. Moreover, while Scripture provides the written testament of divine revelation, it is within the framework of Sacred Tradition that the interpretative and pastoral dimensions unfold, ensuring that the immutable truths remain accessible and comprehensible across ages. This chapter lays the foundation for comprehending how Tradition has not only preserved the integrity of the faith but also allowed it to flourish and adapt in response to the contingencies of history and the needs of humanity, manifesting the enduring presence of the Church as the bride of Christ.

Foundations of Sacred Tradition

To understand the essence of Sacred Tradition within Roman Catholic theology, one must embark on a journey that delves deep into the roots of the Church's teachings and practices. Sacred Tradition is not a mere collection of overgrown customs or folklore; rather, it is regarded as a dynamic and living transmission of the faith, deeply rooted in the apostolic preaching and teachings of Jesus Christ. This tradition is deemed sacred due to its origin and the divine truths it encompasses, serving as a pivotal foundation for the Church's authority and continuity.

At the heart of Sacred Tradition lies the belief that God revealed Himself explicitly through Jesus Christ, whose life and teachings were handed down by the apostles. The Church Fathers, early Christian writers, and theologians such as Tertullian and Origen, emphasized this transmission process while defending the faith against heresies. These early church figures contributed significantly to shaping an understanding that the teachings of Christ, elucidated by the apostles, were preserved not just in written scripture but also through oral traditions, liturgical practices, and the continuous experience of the Christian community.

The significance of Sacred Tradition is also anchored in the idea that the Holy Spirit guides the Church. As articulated during the Council of Trent and reaffirmed in the Second Vatican Council, the Church believes that the Holy Spirit ensures that tradition remains true to the teachings of Christ. This divine guidance is seen as a pivotal element that safeguards the integrity and purity of the faith, enabling the Church to interpret scripture authentically and develop doctrine in a manner consistent with the revealed truths.

The seamless interplay between Sacred Tradition and Sacred Scripture becomes essential when understanding the foundations of Catholic doctrine. St. Paul's epistles, for instance, highlight the importance of holding fast to the teachings delivered both by word of mouth and letter (2 Thessalonians 2:15). This dual mode of transmission—oral and written—reflects the early Church's recognition of the necessity to preserve and pass on the fullness of Christ's teachings. Hence, neither Scripture nor Tradition stands alone; they are interwoven, complementing and elucidating one another, thereby forming a cohesive and comprehensive deposit of faith.

Sacred Tradition manifests in various ways within the life of the Church, from liturgical rites to the doctrinal decrees of ecumenical councils and the writings of the Church Fathers. The practice of liturgy, for example, remains one of the tangible expressions of this tradition. Historical liturgies, drawn from apostolic times, underscore the continuity of worship practices and theological understandings passed down through generations. The divine liturgy is thus more than a ritual; it is a living testimony of the Church's uninterrupted tradition, where each rite and sacrament embodies the truths of faith handed down from the apostles.

Furthermore, the doctrinal formulations of ecumenical councils such as Nicaea, Chalcedon, and Trent serve as monumental testaments to Sacred Tradition. These councils addressed pivotal theological controversies and clarified essential doctrines under the guidance of the Holy Spirit, reflecting a living and dynamic tradition. Such conciliar decrees exemplify how Sacred Tradition operates not as a static relic of the past but as a vibrant and evolving process, continually responding to new questions and challenges while adhering to the apostolic foundations.

The writings of the Church Fathers, such as Augustine, Athanasius, and Gregory the Great, provide another layer of depth to understanding Sacred Tradition. These theological giants engaged in profound reflection, exegesis, and apologetics to articulate the faith's truths more clearly. Their works, which shaped the theological landscape of their times and beyond, are considered integral to the Church's treasure of Sacred Tradition, offering insights and interpretations that remain relevant to contemporary theological discourse.

As the Church journeyed through centuries, Sacred Tradition was critical in encountering various heresies, schisms, and theological disputes. This aspect underscores its role not only in safeguarding doctrinal purity but also in unifying the Church's beliefs and practices. The tradition, continuously scrutinized and affirmed through councils and papal teachings, exemplifies a protective measure against distortions of faith—a beacon that guides the faithful through the complexities of theological inquiries.

Throughout its history, the magisterium, or the teaching office of the Church, has played an essential role in interpreting and preserving Sacred Tradition. The magisterium, consisting of the bishops in communion with the Pope, holds the responsibility of ensuring that the teachings of the Church remain true to the apostolic faith. This authoritative role highlights the communal and hierarchical nature of tradition, where collective discernment and episcopal authority undergird the Church's ability to maintain doctrinal continuity and fidelity.

The Second Vatican Council's *Dei Verbum* (The Dogmatic Constitution on Divine Revelation) provides a definitive articulation of the relationship between Sacred Tradition and Sacred Scripture. The document emphasizes that both Scripture and Tradition flow from the same divine wellspring and aim towards the same goal—communicating the salvific truth of God. According to *Dei Verbum*, they are bound together and communicated in the Church, ensuring that the fullness of God's revelation is conveyed through successive generations.

Dei Verbum also highlights the interpretive role of the magisterium, underlining that without the Church's living tradition, the true meaning of the sacred texts may become obscured. Here, Sacred Tradition acts as a hermeneutical key, unlocking the scriptures' deeper meanings and ensuring their proper understanding within the living faith of the Church. This dynamic interface where tradition and scripture illuminate each other showcases their inseparable union, contributing to a holistic grasp of divine revelation.

The foundational role of Sacred Tradition within Roman Catholic theology is thus multifaceted and profound. It is a testimony of God's continual action in history, manifested through the apostolic preaching, the lived faith experience of the Church, the teachings of the Church Fathers, ecclesiastical decrees, and the liturgical life. Far from being static or redundant, Sacred Tradition signifies a living and ongoing encounter with divine truth, faithfully carried through the Church's journey across millennia.

In conclusion, the foundations of Sacred Tradition reveal a rich tapestry of faith, woven through centuries by the Holy Spirit's guidance. It encompasses more than historical continuity; it signifies a living witness to the revelation of Jesus Christ, preserved and handed down through generations. As theologians, scholars, and believers, our task is to engage with this sacred patrimony, recognizing its profound role in shaping and sustaining the Church's faith and doctrine. This engagement demands continuous reflection, study, and prayer with an acknowledgment of Sacred Tradition as a vital conduit through which the timeless truths of the Catholic faith are elucidated and experienced anew in every age.

Evolution Through the Centuries

The concept of tradition within Roman Catholic theology is not a static entity; instead, it is a dynamic continuum that has evolved over the centuries. This evolution is not merely a chronological progression but rather a theological deepening, influenced by various historical, cultural, and ecclesial contexts. The continuity of tradition is safeguarded by the Magisterium, while its development is propelled by the faithful's ongoing engagement with it.

In the early centuries of the Church, tradition was primarily communicated orally. The apostolic fathers and early councils were instrumental in this phase. They laid down the foundational doctrines and practices that would shape the burgeoning Christian community. The Apostles, who had received their teachings directly from Christ, passed these on to their successors. This "handing down" is the very essence of the word 'tradition,' derived from the Latin "tradere."

The medieval era saw a significant transformation in the understanding and transmission of tradition. The Scholastic period, particularly under the influence of thinkers like St. Thomas Aquinas, integrated Aristotelian philosophy with Christian doctrine. This scholastic synthesis provided a systematic framework for understanding divine revelation. The role of the Church Fathers and Ecumenical Councils was pivotal during this time, as they navigated through heresies and doctrinal disputes to consolidate core theological tenets.

During the Reformation and Counter-Reformation, the concept of tradition faced unprecedented challenges. Protestant reformers like Martin Luther and John Calvin questioned the authority of Church traditions that, in their view, were not rooted in Scripture. In response, the Council of Trent (1545-1563) emphatically reaffirmed the dual sources of divine revelation: Sacred Scripture and Sacred Tradition. This period highlighted the Church's resilience in upholding tradition amid external critiques and internal reforms.

The Enlightenment and modernity brought new intellectual currents that impacted the Church's understanding of tradition. Reason and empirical sciences began to take precedence, challenging the Church to articulate its teachings in this new paradigm. The First Vatican Council (1869-1870) and later the Second Vatican Council (1962-1965) played crucial roles in re-contextualizing tradition within contemporary thought. Vatican II, in particular, emphasized the living nature of tradition, portraying it as a dynamic process that involves growth and development while remaining faithful to its apostolic roots.

In modern times, theologians such as Yves Congar and Hans Küng have further enriched our understanding of tradition. Congar, with his emphasis on the Church's pneumatological dimension, illustrated how the Holy Spirit continuously breathes life into tradition. Küng, on the other hand, brought attention to the critical engagement with tradition, showing how it must be continually scrutinized and reinterpreted to remain relevant.

One of the great challenges of our age is reconciling the immutable and eternal truths of divine revelation with the evolving contexts in which the Church finds herself. The living tradition of the Church must balance the tension between fidelity to the apostolic faith and responsiveness to modern existential realities. This dynamic interplay ensures that tradition is not a mere relic of the past but a vibrant and life-giving force.

The role of the Magisterium remains crucial in this evolutionary process. The teaching authority of the Church serves as the guardian and interpreter of tradition, ensuring that developments remain coherent with the deposit of faith. However, the faithful's sensus fidei, or sense of the faith, also plays a vital role. It is through the lived experience of the faithful that tradition finds its fullest expression and relevance.

As we move forward, the evolution of tradition faces both challenges and opportunities. In a rapidly changing world, the Church must discern how to navigate issues such as globalization, technological advancements, and shifting cultural norms. Yet, these challenges also provide opportunities to deepen and enrich the understanding of tradition, showing its perennial relevance and transformative power.

In conclusion, the evolution of tradition through the centuries is a testament to the Church's capacity to adapt and grow while remaining anchored in the foundational truths of the faith. This continuous development, guided by the Holy Spirit, ensures that tradition remains a living and active expression of divine revelation, ever capable of enlightening and guiding the faithful in their journey toward God.

Chapter 2: Yves Congar's Perspective on Tradition

Stepping into the rich tapestry of Yves Congar's theological insights, we find a profound and nuanced understanding of tradition, which he considered the lifeblood of the Church. For Congar, tradition wasn't just a static inheritance from the past but a dynamic and living reality, through which the Holy Spirit continues to work in the Church today. His vision encompassed an organic development, suggesting that tradition grows and unfolds much like a living organism, guided by the same Spirit that inspired the Scriptures. Congar's perspective was deeply rooted in his early influences and theological background, which he skillfully wove into his key contributions. He emphasized the necessity of distinguishing between "Tradition" (with a capital T), representing the core truths of the faith handed down from the apostles, and "traditions" (lowercase t), which are the various practices and expressions that can change over time. His efforts to clarify and harmonize these aspects reflect a balance between fidelity to the past and openness to the present, making his contribution invaluable for contemporary theology.

Early Influences and Theological Background

Yves Congar, a towering figure in the realm of 20th-century Catholic theology, was deeply shaped by his early experiences and the theological milieu in which he was immersed. Born in Sedan, France, in 1904, Congar's formative years were marked by the upheavals of World War I. His family's displacement and the experiences during the war left an indelible impression on him, fostering a sense of resilience and a commitment to reconciliation and unity, which would later permeate his ecclesiological vision.

Congar's theological education began at the seminary in Rheims, and later at the Institut Catholique de Paris, where he was influenced by the neoscholasticism prevailing at the time. However, his intellectual curiosity led him beyond the confines of neoscholastic thought. He delved deeply into the works of the Church Fathers, particularly the writings of Augustine and the Eastern Fathers, which significantly impacted his understanding of tradition and its development.

The period he spent in Rome further enriched his theological perspective. It was here that Congar encountered Thomism in a more profound way, particularly the works of Thomas Aquinas. Aquinas's synthesis of faith and reason, his robust metaphysical framework, and his profound insights into the nature of the Church provided Congar with tools to articulate his own theological vision.

A turning point in Congar's theological journey was his association with the Dominican Order. Entering the novitiate at Amiens in 1925, Congar embraced the order's intellectual rigor and commitment to study and teaching. The Dominican emphasis on 'contemplata aliis tradere' – to give to others the fruits of contemplation – resonated deeply with Congar's own burgeoning sense of vocation.

One cannot overlook the influence of the French ressourcement movement on Congar. This movement, which sought to return to the sources of Christian thought – the Scriptures and the writings of the early

Church Fathers – was a reaction against the perceived aridness of neo-scholasticism. Congar, along with other theologians such as Henri de Lubac and Jean Daniélou, sought to rejuvenate Catholic theology by retrieving its ancient roots. This endeavor was not merely an academic exercise but was seen as essential for the renewal of the Church.

In addition to the ressourcement movement, Congar's thought was profoundly shaped by historical-critical studies of the Bible and Tradition. The emerging field of Biblical studies, which applied historical-critical methods to the Scriptures, provided Congar with new insights into the dynamic and living nature of Tradition. He came to see Tradition not as a static deposit but as a living reality that unfolds and develops over time, guided by the Holy Spirit.

Ecumenism also played a crucial role in Congar's theological development. His experiences during World War II, particularly his time in German captivity, brought him into contact with Protestant pastors and theologians. These encounters fostered in him a deep commitment to Christian unity and a recognition of the richness of other Christian traditions. Congar's work in ecumenism, particularly his involvement in the World Council of Churches, underscored his belief that the division among Christians was a scandal and that genuine dialogue was essential for the unity of the Church.

Central to Congar's understanding of tradition were his engagements with ecclesiology. For Congar, the Church was not merely an institution but a living body, the People of God, journeying through history. He was profoundly influenced by the ecclesiological insights of theologians like Johann Adam Möhler and by the Eastern Orthodox understanding of the Church as a communion. This ecclesiological vision informed his understanding of Tradition as something dynamic, communal, and deeply rooted in the life of the Church.

During his career, Congar's positions often put him at odds with the ecclesiastical authorities. His support for liturgical reforms and a more collegial governance of the Church, coupled with his views on Tradition, led to periods of marginalization. Yet, Congar persisted, driven by a profound love for the Church and a conviction that reform was essential for its fidelity to the Gospel.

Congar's theological journey is also marked by his experiences at the Second Vatican Council (1962-1965). As a peritus (theological expert), Congar played a significant role in shaping many of the council's key documents, particularly those related to the Church, ecumenism, and revelation. The council's emphasis on returning to the sources (aggiornamento) and its recognition of the dynamic nature of Tradition was deeply influenced by Congar's thought.

Throughout his life, Congar remained committed to a theology that was both faithful to the tradition of the Church and responsive to the signs of the times. His early influences, from his wartime experiences to his academic formation, shaped a theologian who was deeply committed to the renewal and unity of the Church. Congar's theological background, enriched by his engagements with Scripture, the Church Fathers, Thomism, and ecumenism, provided him with a unique perspective on Tradition – one that continues to resonate in contemporary theological discussions.

Key Contributions to Understanding Tradition

Yves Congar, a Dominican friar and one of the most pivotal theologians of the 20th century, contributed significantly to the Catholic Church's understanding of Tradition. His insights have shaped contemporary theological discourse and continue to influence scholars and practitioners alike. Congar's work can be seen as a bridge that connects ancient truths with modern expressions, providing clarity and context to the complex concept of Tradition.

One of Congar's key contributions lies in his strong emphasis on the dynamic and living nature of Tradition. He argued that Tradition is not a static deposit of faith handed down mechanically but a living reality that grows and develops within the life of the Church. This idea sought to counteract any overly rigid interpretations that might stifle the living Spirit at work within the Church. By describing Tradition as a dynamic process, Congar allowed theologians and the faithful to appreciate the organic unity between past revelations and the Church's continuous journey through history.

Congar also elaborated on the relationship between Scripture and Tradition, asserting that both are integral and inseparable parts of the same divine revelation. He stressed that Scripture itself is a product of Tradition, formulated and canonized by the early Church fathers within the context of the community's lived experience. This viewpoint challenges any notion that the Bible alone (sola scriptura) can encapsulate the entirety of divine revelation without acknowledging the broader framework of Tradition in which it operates.

Another significant aspect of Congar's work is his focus on the ecclesiological dimensions of Tradition. He believed that Tradition was inherently tied to the Church's understanding of itself and its mission. The Church, as the "Body of Christ," is both the guardian and the interpreter of Tradition. Congar underlined the role of the Magisterium—the Church's teaching authority—in safeguarding and elucidating this Tradition. However, he also championed the idea of "reception," where the faithful collectively participate in the discernment and acceptance of Tradition, ensuring it remains relevant and meaningful.

Congar's contributions also extend to his notion of "ressourcement," a term he used to describe the process of returning to the sources of Christian faith, particularly the Scriptures and the early Church Fathers. This return to the origins was not meant to be a retreat into the past but rather a way to rejuvenate and renew the Church's understanding of its Tradition. By advocating for ressourcement, Congar provided a methodological framework that enabled theologians to engage creatively and faithfully with the foundational texts and traditions of Christianity.

Furthermore, Congar's ecumenical sensitivity is another cornerstone of his understanding of Tradition. He was deeply committed to the reunification of Christian denominations and believed that a proper appreciation of Tradition could serve as a bridge rather than a barrier. His work in ecumenism highlighted the shared theological and historical roots that different Christian traditions hold, allowing for greater dialogue and potential reconciliation. By framing Tradition as a common heritage, Congar hoped to foster a more inclusive and cooperative Christian witness.

In addition to his theological insights, Congar's historical consciousness played a significant role in his interpretation of Tradition. He was acutely aware of the historical developments and shifts within the Church and aimed to account for these changes in his theological method. This historical awareness provided a nuanced understanding of Tradition as something that is both received and developed over time, subject to the influences and contexts of different historical periods. Congar's historically informed approach helps contemporary theologians appreciate the complexities and layers of Tradition without falling into the trap of anachronism or oversimplification.

Congar's emphasis on the pastoral implications of Tradition cannot be overstated. He always maintained that theological principles should not remain confined to academic discourse but must be translated into the life and practice of the Church. He saw Tradition as something that must inform and enrich the pastoral activities of the Church, guiding the faithful in their spiritual journey. This pastoral sensitivity ensured that Congar's theological insights were accessible and practical, capable of addressing the concerns and needs of ordinary believers.

Moreover, Yves Congar's work addressed the concept of "Tradition and traditions," making a distinction between the core, essential elements of the faith and the various cultural and liturgical practices that have developed over the centuries. This distinction allowed him to advocate for a more flexible and adaptable approach to Tradition, where essential truths remain consistent while secondary traditions can evolve and change. This concept has proven vital in contemporary discussions on inculturation and the adaptation of the Gospel message to diverse cultural contexts.

In summary, Yves Congar's contributions to understanding Tradition are vast and multi-faceted. He offered a vision of Tradition as a living, dynamic reality deeply embedded within the life of the Church. His nuanced perspectives on Scripture and Tradition, ecclesiology, ressourcement, ecumenism, historical consciousness, and pastoral application have profoundly influenced Catholic theology and continue to shape the Church's engagement with its sacred heritage. Engaging with Congar's work allows for a deeper appreciation of the richness and complexity of Tradition, inviting theologians, Church leaders, and the faithful to participate more fully in the ongoing journey of faith.

Chapter 3: Hans Küng's Approach to Tradition

Hans Küng's approach to tradition within Roman Catholic theology is characterized by a critical and innovative examination, challenging established norms while remaining deeply rooted in the historical context of the Church. His theological journey, influenced by both classical scholarship and contemporary philosophical thought, prompts a re-evaluation of tradition not as a static inheritance but as a dynamic, evolving narrative. Küng emphasizes the necessity of an open dialogue with modernity, advocating for a living tradition that interacts actively with the changing human experience without compromising its foundational truths. His critiques, often controversial and subject to ecclesiastical scrutiny, underscore the tension between adhering to historical continuity and addressing current existential realities. Ultimately, Küng seeks a balance where tradition inspires and informs but does not constrain, encouraging a faith that is both historically grounded and profoundly relevant.

Influences and Theological Foundations

Hans Küng's theological framework is heavily anchored in the kaleidoscopic heritage of Catholic tradition, yet it unflinchingly explores the intricate puzzle pieces that compose it. Küng's scholastic journey draws influence from both ancient and contemporary theological paradigms, positioning his approach at a unique crossroads. This cross-pollination of ideas has fostered a nuanced understanding of the living tradition. But what are the forces that shaped his perspectives?

First and foremost, Küng's theological lens is significantly informed by his rigorous examination of early Church Fathers. Figures like Augustine and Origen offer a foundational layer to his theology. These early theologians grappled with weaving complex doctrines into a coherent faith narrative, much like Küng himself would attempt centuries later. Augustine's emphasis on God's immeasurability and Origen's allegorical interpretations of scripture illustrate an approach to mystery that Küng found invaluable.

Moreover, Küng was influenced by the theological ethos emanating from the Scholastic period. St. Thomas Aquinas' systematic approach to faith and reason created a matrix that would greatly impact Küng's intellectual pursuits. The synthesis of Aristotelian philosophy with Christian theology provided a robust framework for tackling the dual realms of faith and rational inquiry. Aquinas' dedication to understanding faith through reason offered a stabilizing counterbalance to the more mystical dimensions present in earlier Christian writings.

In addition to classical influences, modern theological movements also played a vital role in shaping Küng's perspectives. Yves Congar, a contemporary and fellow theologian, exerted a significant influence. Congar's ecclesiological innovations and focus on the Church as a living community resonated deeply with Küng. Both theologians shared a commitment to reforming the Church from within, emphasizing a return to the original sources of Christian theology.

Furthermore, Karl Barth's dialectical theology permeates Küng's work, exemplifying the tension between divine revelation and human understanding. Barth's emphasis on the transcendence of God and the centrality of Christ in theological discourse became pivotal in Küng's approach. This Christocentric focus can be traced through much of Küng's writings, reflecting Barth's insistence on the supreme role of Jesus Christ in revealing God's essence.

Küng's educational background, particularly his time at the Pontifical Gregorian University in Rome and later studies at the University of Paris, also provided fertile ground for his theological explorations. These institutions exposed him to diverse theological traditions and methods, further enhancing his ability to engage with tradition in a critically constructive manner.

More than just academic influences, the cultural and societal context of the 20th century profoundly impacted Küng's theological orientation. The existential crises of two World Wars, the rise of secularism, and the transformative period of Vatican II all played roles in shaping his thought. Vatican II, in particular, was a watershed moment for Küng, fostering an environment ripe for ecclesiological and liturgical renewal.

During Vatican II, Küng was an advocate for aggiornamento — the updating and renewal of the Church. His advocacy for returning to foundational texts and purging accretions that he deemed unfaithful to the original Christian message was a clarion call for reform. This approach was not without controversy but reveals Küng's commitment to a living, dynamic tradition that is continuously reinterpreted in light of contemporary contexts.

Küng's theological journey was also shaped by his engagement with Protestant theology. He worked closely with Protestant thinkers and appreciated their emphasis on scripture's primacy. This ecumenical spirit underscored his theological work, aiming to bridge the chasms between Catholic and Protestant traditions.

By exploring these diverse influences, Küng constructed a theological methodology grounded in historical awareness yet responsive to contemporary challenges. His approach to tradition was both an act of preservation and innovation. In doing so, he underscored the necessity of engaging critically and creatively with the received tradition.

One of Küng's distinguished methods was his hermeneutical approach — the art and science of interpretation. Embracing a hermeneutic of trust rather than suspicion, he delved into historical texts with both reverence and critical inquiry. This balance allowed him to engage deeply with the tradition while also seeking out genuine reforms within it.

Küng's hermeneutics was also closely aligned with philosophical currents of his time. He was particularly influenced by the existentialist and phenomenological traditions, which emphasize human experience and perception. Thinkers like Martin Heidegger and Hans-Georg Gadamer offered Küng tools for understanding how human beings encounter the divine in historical and cultural contexts. This philosophical background informed his theological interpretations, making his approach uniquely comprehensive.

Another key influence on Küng's thought was liberation theology, especially its focus on social justice and the preferential option for the poor. This alignment with liberation theology highlighted his commitment to a faith that is not only doctrinally sound but also practically engaged with the world's sufferings. The notion that theological reflection must lead to practical, ethical action resonated deeply with Küng's overall project.

In synthesizing these various influences, Küng developed a theology that was critically engaged with tradition, yet dynamically open to reform. His commitment to both historical rootedness and contemporary relevance underscored his work, offering a model for engaging with the enduring truths of faith while facing the ever-evolving challenges of modernity.

In conclusion, Küng's approach to tradition is a rich tapestry woven from diverse influences ranging from early Church Fathers to contemporary theologians and cultural contexts. By critically engaging with these myriad sources, he developed a theological methodology that is both rooted and reformist, providing vital insights into the living tradition of the Church. Through Küng, we see how theological foundations can be both a source of stability and a springboard for transformative change.

Controversies and Criticisms

Hans Küng, a notable theological figure, has been a subject of intense debate within the Roman Catholic Church, especially regarding his approach to tradition. His perspectives stirred academic circles and ecclesiastical authorities alike, prompting both admiration and criticism. Küng's approach to tradition, particularly his views on ecclesiastical authority and papal infallibility, has been at the forefront of these controversies.

Küng questioned some deeply entrenched beliefs within Roman Catholicism, particularly those concerning the infallibility of the Pope. He argued that the doctrine was not only problematic but also not explicitly supported by early Christian tradition. This stance placed him at odds with the magisterium and led to significant friction within the Church hierarchy. Critics accused Küng of undermining the Church's authority, suggesting that his views could lead to theological anarchy.

More than any other doctrine, Küng's critique of papal infallibility drew the most substantial ire. He argued that the First Vatican Council's (1869-1870) declaration of papal infallibility lacked sufficient historical foundation. This assertion brought him directly into conflict with the magisterium, which considered the doctrine a cornerstone of Catholic teaching. His critics assert that by challenging this doctrine, Küng indirectly questioned the Church's ability to safeguard divine truth through its tradition.

Adding to the contention, Küng's methodology was distinct from traditional theological approaches. He often employed historical-critical methods, which some considered too secular and inappropriate for sacred theology. Rather than taking the established teachings at face value, he scrutinized them through the lens of historical development and social context. Detractors claimed this approach eroded the mystical and timeless nature of sacred tradition, reducing it to merely a historical phenomenon.

Küng's insistence on reform and modernization within the Church further fueled criticism. He advocated for a re-evaluation of age-old traditions in the light of contemporary issues and scientific advancements. Küng emphasized that tradition should not be static; instead, it should evolve to meet the changing needs of the faithful. Opponents argued that this perspective risked diluting the faith, making it subject to the whims of transient societal trends rather than anchoring it in perennial truths.

Another point of contention was Küng's view on ecumenism. He held that interfaith dialogue and unity among Christian denominations required a critical reassessment of traditional doctrines. This stance, while progressive and aimed at bridging gaps, was met with skepticism and resistance from traditionalists who saw it as compromising core Catholic tenets. Critics contended that Küng's openness to ecumenical dialogue could potentially dilute the unique doctrines that set Roman Catholicism apart from other Christian traditions.

The controversy surrounding Küng extended beyond theological circles into broader ecclesiastical affairs. His critical perspectives eventually led to disciplinary action from the Vatican. In 1979, the Congregation for the Doctrine of the Faith, then led by Cardinal Joseph Ratzinger (later Pope Benedict XVI), revoked Küng's license to teach Catholic theology. This move was both lauded and lamented. Supporters cheered it as a necessary measure to protect doctrinal purity, while critics decried it as an instance of intellectual repression.

Despite the institutional backlash, Küng retained significant support among many theologians, scholars, and laypeople who admired his courage and commitment to reform. These supporters viewed him as a prophetic voice, challenging outdated practices and advocating for a more inclusive and modern Church. They saw his critiques not as attacks on the Church but as necessary steps towards its renewal and relevance in the modern world.

Moreover, critics often disregarded the nuance in Küng's arguments. While he questioned certain doctrines, he remained deeply committed to the core of the Christian faith. His criticisms were aimed at what he perceived to be historical additions rather than the essential truths of the

Gospel. For Küng, a genuine adherence to tradition meant continuously revisiting and interpreting it in light of new understandings and challenges.

Küng's critics also targeted his approach to scriptural interpretation. He often argued for a more dynamic interplay between scripture and tradition, contending that scripture could offer new insights when tradition was critically examined and vice versa. This was seen by traditionalists as undermining the established exegetical methods and the magisterial interpretations that had guided the Church for centuries. They feared that such an approach could lead to relativism, where doctrines were continuously up for debate rather than being seen as divine mandates.

In conclusion, Hans Küng's approach to tradition, which questioned long-held doctrines and advocated for a historical-critical method, garnered both significant criticism and robust support. While his detractors saw his views as a threat to the stability and authority of the Church, his supporters viewed him as a necessary reformer, urging the Church to evolve and remain relevant in contemporary society. The controversies and criticisms surrounding Küng's work underscore the persistent struggle within the Catholic Church to balance tradition with the pressing needs of the modern era.

Chapter 4: Tradition and Sacred Scripture

Tradition and Sacred Scripture form the dual pillars upon which Catholic theology rests, intricately woven together through the centuries to guide the faithful in discerning divine truths. The interaction between these two sources of revelation is not merely historical but also theological, demonstrating a symbiotic relationship that underscores the Church's mission to faithfully transmit God's word. In examining their interplay, one sees how Tradition serves as the living context within which Sacred Scripture is both interpreted and understood; it encapsulates the collective wisdom and spiritual insights accumulated through generations of ecclesiastical teaching and practice. The historical development and canon formation of the Scriptures further illustrate this dynamic, where the Church, guided by the Holy Spirit, discerned the inspired texts that accurately reflect apostolic faith. This process highlights the inherent unity between Scripture, Tradition, and the Magisterium, ensuring that the immutable truths of God remain accessible to humanity through His Bride, the Church. Thus, the enduring legacy of Tradition and Sacred Scripture continues to illuminate the path of the faithful, bridging the temporal with the eternal.

Interplay Between Scripture and Tradition

The intricate dance between Scripture and Tradition is a cornerstone of Roman Catholic theology. This interplay is foundational for understanding how Divine Revelation has been transmitted through the ages. Distinct yet inseparable, Scripture and Tradition have worked in concert to unveil the immutable truths contained within God's message to humanity. Scripture holds the written word, while Tradition embodies the living experience of faith, manifesting through teachings, liturgical practices, and historical events that have been faithfully passed down from one generation to the next.

To adequately comprehend this interplay, it's essential to recognize that Sacred Tradition preceded the canonization of Sacred Scripture. The early Christian community operated primarily within an oral culture, relying heavily on the spoken word and the lived experience of those who were direct witnesses to Jesus Christ's ministry. Tradition preserved these teachings before they were ever committed to text. In this sense, Tradition nurtured Scripture, preparing the fertile ground into which the seed of the written Word would be planted.

One of the defining moments in the relationship between Scripture and Tradition can be traced back to the Councils that determined the canon of the Bible. These ecclesiastical gatherings were guided by the Holy Spirit, using the criteria provided by Tradition—such as apostolic origin and consistent usage in liturgy—to discern which writings were genuinely inspired. Consequently, the canon of Scripture reflects the mind of the Church, rooted in the living Tradition, which serves as an interpretative key for the Biblical texts.

The symbiotic nature of Scripture and Tradition is perhaps most evident in the liturgy. The liturgical practices of the Church are steeped in Scripture; the words of the Bible permeate every aspect of the Mass. At the same time, the Tradition of how the liturgy is performed provides a context that deeper illuminates the meaning of the scriptural passages. This mutual enhancement underscores the notion that neither Scripture nor Tradition can stand fully in isolation, each reliant on the other to fully convey the richness of God's revelation.

The role of the Magisterium, the Church's teaching authority, is crucial in maintaining this delicate balance. The Magisterium, consisting of the Pope and the bishops in communion with him, serves as the custodian and interpreter of both Scripture and Tradition. By discerning and declaring the authentic teachings, the Magisterium ensures continuity and consistency in faith and morals across the centuries. The Church Fathers and subsequent theologians have long echoed this sentiment, emphasizing that the integrity of Doctrine is preserved through this venerable triad of Scripture, Tradition, and the Magisterium.

Furthermore, the interplay between Scripture and Tradition is evident in the development of Christian doctrine. Doctrinal formulations often emerge as reflections on the sacred texts, enlightened by the lived experience and divine insights carried through Tradition. Historical examples such as the Nicene Creed illustrate how Tradition provides the framework within which Scripture is interpreted, ensuring that doctrines remain faithful to the apostolic faith. These doctrinal developments are not seen as innovations but as organic growths sprouting from the same root.

In addressing the contemporary context, it's beneficial to look at the Second Vatican Council, a significant moment that encapsulated the ongoing dialogue between Scripture and Tradition. The Council's document "Dei Verbum" is particularly emphatic in articulating that "Sacred Tradition and Sacred Scripture form one sacred deposit of the word of God, committed to the Church." This conciliar emphasis reaffirmed that Scripture and Tradition are not parallel or competing sources but a united and equitable fountain of divine revelation.

The nuances in understanding Scripture through Tradition can also be observed in the practice of exegesis. The exegetical tradition in the Church doesn't merely seek to uncover the historical and literal meanings of the text. Instead, it endeavors to understand the spiritual sense, a task requiring insights from the broader Tradition. Patristic writings, councils, and liturgical texts provide a hermeneutical lens, allowing deeper insights into the scriptural passages' full theological significance. This rich tapestry ensures that the scriptures are vibrant and relevant to the contemporary faithful's spiritual and moral lives.

Moreover, Tradition and Scripture work together to provide responses to theological controversies and heresies. Throughout history, periods of doctrinal ambiguity or challenge have consistently been resolved by invoking the deeply rooted Tradition of the Church alongside the scriptural texts. Examples include the early Christological controversies, where the formulations of the Councils of Nicaea and Chalcedon drew heavily upon both Scripture and the interpretative Tradition maintained by the preceding centuries of the Church's life.

It would be remiss not to consider the organic and dynamic nature of Tradition within the Church. Tradition is not static; it's a living transmission. This vitality derives from the Holy Spirit, who continues to guide the Church. Consequently, Tradition is dynamic, always in dialogue with the evolving understanding and practices within the Church, yet firmly anchored within the foundational truths revealed in Scripture. This dynamism ensures that Tradition remains relevant and resonates with each new generation without deviating from its apostolic origins.

It's evident that both Scripture and Tradition find their unity and fullness in the person of Jesus Christ. As the Word made flesh, Christ is the ultimate revelation of the Father, and it is through Him that both Scripture and Tradition draw their life and coherence. Therefore, the ultimate purpose of this interplay is not merely to preserve a compendium of teachings or practices but to bring the faithful into an ever-deepening communion with Christ Himself.

In sum, the relationship between Scripture and Tradition is one of profound interdependence. Far from being mere historical relics, they are dynamic, living realities that collaborate in the ever-unfolding revelation of God's timeless truth. To separate them is to diminish the fullness of the faith they jointly proclaim. As theologians, scholars, and believers continue to delve into the depths of this interplay, they find a faith that is not only rooted in history but also ever pertinent to the contemporary journey of striving toward divine wisdom.

Historical Development and Canon Formation

The historical development of the canon of Sacred Scripture in the Roman Catholic tradition is a narrative interwoven with the threads of historical events, theological reflections, and ecclesiastical decisions. The process of recognizing and formalizing the biblical canon was neither instantaneous nor marked by a singular, decisive event. Instead, it was a gradual unfolding, deeply rooted in the life and worship of the early Christian communities.

In the earliest days of the Church, the first Christians relied on the Hebrew Scriptures, what we now call the Old Testament. These texts were an integral part of the liturgical and communal life of the nascent Christian faith. The teachings of Jesus, as recorded by the apostles, were initially passed down orally, forming a vital part of the Sacred Tradition. It wasn't until the mid-1st century that written accounts began to emerge, as the apostles composed letters and gospels to address the needs and questions of the growing Christian communities.

The process of determining which texts were to be considered authoritative and which were to be excluded was influenced by various factors, including apostolic authorship, consistency with the rule of faith, and widespread acceptance among the Christian communities. In this endeavor, the early Church Fathers played a crucial role. They evaluated the emerging scriptures through the lens of the apostolic tradition, ensuring that the core teachings of Christ and His apostles were preserved.

By the late 2nd century, figures such as Irenaeus of Lyons and Tertullian began referencing a set of texts that would later be recognized as the New Testament. However, this emerging canon was not without contention. Different communities favored different texts, and various fringe writings, known as apocrypha, vied for acceptance. The discernment process involved vigorous debates and discernment guided by the Holy Spirit, and the final selections were scenarios of both controversy and consensus.

Formal recognition of the canonical books came through ecclesiastical councils. The Council of Rome in 382 AD, under Pope Damasus I, provided one of the earliest lists of canonical books that correspond closely to what we have today in the New Testament. This list was further affirmed and ratified by subsequent councils: the Synods of Hippo (393 AD) and Carthage (397 and 419 AD). These councils' decisions were crucial not merely for establishing a biblical canon but also for reinforcing the unity of doctrine within the Church.

During these formative years, the canon was solidified by a combination of ecclesiastical authority and the lived experience of the faithful. The efforts of early Church Fathers, bishops, and councils were all part of a dynamic crystallization process in which the Sacred Tradition and written Scriptures were seen as complementary facets of divine revelation. The interdependence of Tradition and Scripture cannot be overstated; the Tradition provided the necessary context and interpretative keys to understand the Scriptures correctly.

Moving into the medieval period, the canon of the Bible continued to be referenced and utilized within the theological and liturgical frameworks of the Church. During this epoch, scholastics like Thomas Aquinas engaged deeply with the Scriptures, seeking to harmonize reason and faith. The texts recognized as canonical continued to serve as the foundation for theological exploration and doctrinal development.

The advent of the Reformation in the 16th century brought fresh challenges to the established canon. Protestant reformers questioned the inclusion of certain Old Testament books, known as the deuterocanonical books, and advocated for a return to the Hebrew Masoretic Text's canon. In response, the Counter-Reformation and the Council of Trent (1545-1563) reaffirmed the canonicity of these disputed books and emphasized the importance of Tradition in interpreting Scripture.

The Council of Trent declared that the Church's authority unveiled the correct canon, guiding believers away from private interpretation that could diverge from the apostolic faith. This reaffirmation was not merely a reactionary stance but a re-emphasis on the coherent unity of Scripture and Tradition, essential for maintaining doctrinal orthodoxy. The

Church's magisterial role was underscored as the authentic interpreter and guardian of the biblical texts, entrusted with preserving the integrity of its teachings.

In the modern era, the Second Vatican Council (1962-1965) revisited the relationship between Scripture and Tradition in the document *Dei Verbum*. This Dogmatic Constitution on Divine Revelation articulated a renewed understanding that both sacred Tradition and sacred Scripture flow from the same divine wellspring. It emphasized that Scripture must be read within the living Tradition of the whole Church, highlighting an integrative approach to divine revelation.

As we survey the development of the canon, it becomes evident that it is not merely a historical artifact but a living testimony to the Church's faith journey. The development of the canon stands as a testament to the Church's fidelity to its apostolic origins while navigating the complexities and challenges across centuries. The canonization process was both a human endeavor, characterized by discernment, debate, and decision, and a divine undertaking, guided by the Holy Spirit.

Understanding the historical development and canon formation reminds us that the Scriptures are not isolated texts but are dynamically integrated into the Church's life. This integration invites us, even today, to approach the Bible not solely as a historical document but as a living sacramental text, ever vibrant within the context of Tradition and the Church's teaching authority.

In conclusion, the formation of the biblical canon is a profound instance of the Church's reliance on Tradition to discern and articulate the divine revelation contained within Scripture. This intricate process allowed for a cohesive, communal understanding of God's word, ensuring that the faith delivered to the apostles would be faithfully transmitted throughout the ages. The journey of canon development underscores the importance of the interplay between Tradition and Scripture, a relationship pivotal for comprehending immutable and eternal truths revealed by God and embraced by His bride, the Church.

Chapter 5: Tradition in the Early Apostolic Church

The nuances of Christian Tradition found their earliest foothold in the lives and writings of the Apostolic Fathers and the initial ecclesiastical assemblies. Within these formative years, doctrines were not just verbal articulations but were interwoven with the community's lived experiences, shaped through a symbiotic relationship with Sacred Scripture and the oral teachings of the apostles. The Apostolic Fathers, with their firsthand connections to the Apostles, became the custodians of these traditions, ensuring the transmission of Christ's teachings against a backdrop of emerging heresies and diverse interpretations. This period witnessed the foundational development of doctrine, where the nascent Church, guided by the Holy Spirit, began to formally articulate its faith through creeds and the discernment of canonical texts. It was a time marked by a fervent commitment to preserving the apostolic witness and the gradual structuring of ecclesial authority through synods and early councils. Herein lies the genesis of a living Tradition, molding the future contours of Christian orthodoxy and praxis.

Apostolic Fathers and Early Councils

The Apostolic Fathers, those Christian theologians who lived in the first and early second centuries, represent the foundational link between the Apostles and subsequent generations of Church leaders. Their works convey an evolving understanding of the nascent faith, one that was deeply rooted in the teachings of the Apostles yet adapted to the challenges and contexts of their time. These revered figures, such as Clement of Rome, Ignatius of Antioch, and Polycarp of Smyrna, not only served as pastoral leaders but also as crucial transmitters of apostolic truth, embodying and elucidating the principles of Sacred Tradition.

Their writings, often composed in the form of epistles or homilies, delve into essential doctrinal and pastoral issues. For instance, Clement's letter to the Corinthians addresses ecclesiastical hierarchy and the importance of maintaining unity, revealing early concerns about schism and the preservation of apostolic authority. Ignatius, through his epistles written en route to martyrdom in Rome, emphasizes the centrality of the Eucharist and the role of the bishop as a locus of unity and orthodoxy, prefiguring later ecclesiological developments.

Polycarp, a disciple of the Apostle John, serves as another vital conduit of apostolic teachings. His martyrdom reinforces the theme of unwavering fidelity to Christ and the doctrinal purity passed down from the Apostles. These figures, in their lives and writings, reflect a Church grappling with external pressures, such as Roman persecution, and internal challenges, including heretical movements like Gnosticism.

The Apostolic Fathers not only preserved apostolic doctrine but also engaged in the development of a coherent ecclesial structure. This period witnesses an increasing delineation of clerical roles and the articulation of ecclesiastical authority, elements that would become definitive features of the Christian tradition. Their efforts were instrumental in setting the stage for the doctrinal and structural consolidations that would follow in the early councils.

Turning to the early ecumenical councils, these were assemblies where bishops and church leaders gathered to resolve theological disputes and affirm orthodox doctrine. The necessity of these councils emerged from the growing diversity of thought within early Christianity and the need for a unified theological front. The first of these, the Council of Nicaea in 325 AD, addressed the Arian controversy, which questioned the divinity of Christ. By affirming the consubstantiality of the Son with the Father, the Nicene Creed established a cornerstone for Trinitarian theology and underscored the authority of ecumenical decisions in defining orthodoxy.

Subsequent councils, such as those at Constantinople (381 AD) and Chalcedon (451 AD), continued this work, tackling Christological controversies that revolved around the nature and person of Christ. The Council of Constantinople expanded the Nicene Creed, adding clauses to clarify the divinity of the Holy Spirit, while Chalcedon provided a definitive expression of Christ's dual natures, both fully divine and fully human, in the hypostatic union. Through these councils, the Church endeavored not only to expound upon the apostolic faith but also to address heresies that threatened the unity and integrity of Christian doctrine.

These early councils were not only theological in nature but also deeply pastoral, seeking to guide the faithful through periods of doctrinal confusion and conflict. They underscore the Church's reliance on Sacred Tradition to interpret and clarify the faith handed down from the Apostles. The acts and decrees of these councils, often ratified through creeds and canons, exhibit a profound interplay between Tradition and emerging theological articulations.

It's imperative to recognize the inherent link between the Apostolic Fathers and these councils. The foundational work of the Apostolic Fathers laid the groundwork for the conciliar developments that followed. Their writings and teachings provided a repository of apostolic truth, which the councils drew upon in formulating their doctrinal definitions. This continuity of Tradition, from the apostolic era through the early councils, highlights the Church's commitment to preserving and faithfully transmitting the core tenets of the Christian faith.

The significance of the Apostolic Fathers and the early councils in shaping the trajectory of Christian doctrine cannot be overstated. They represent a period of vigorous theological activity and consolidation, wherein the Church sought to define its beliefs and practices in the face of internal and external challenges. By engaging with heresies and controversies through the lens of Tradition, these early Christian leaders and assemblies forged a path towards doctrinal clarity and ecclesial unity.

Moreover, the decisions and teachings of the Apostolic Fathers and the early councils continue to resonate throughout the centuries. They serve as touchstones for subsequent theological reflection and ecclesiastical governance, ensuring that the faith of the Apostles remains a living and dynamic tradition. In this regard, the early phase of Tradition exemplified by these figures and gatherings provides a blueprint for understanding the Church's ongoing endeavor to faithfully transmit the depositum fidei across generations.

In conclusion, the Apostolic Fathers and early councils are pivotal in the historical and theological development of Sacred Tradition. Their contributions illuminate the Church's early efforts to preserve and explicate the apostolic faith, laying the foundation for the rich and complex tradition that would continue to evolve throughout Christian history. Their legacy, enshrined in both their writings and the decrees of the councils, remains a testament to the enduring power and significance of Tradition in the life of the Catholic Church.

Development of Christian Doctrine

In the burgeoning days of the Early Apostolic Church, the seeds of what would become established Christian doctrine were sown with a blend of fervent faith and measured contemplation. Church leaders, many of whom had been direct disciples of Christ or His immediate followers, sought to preserve and propagate the teachings they had received. Their endeavor was not merely to adhere to a set of rules but to foster an organic, living faith that could be passed down through the generations. This transitional phase was crucial in shaping the trajectory of Christian doctrine, and it is here that Sacred Tradition found fertile ground to flourish.

The Apostolic Fathers, including figures like Clement of Rome and Polycarp, along with early councils, played an indelible role in this formative period. These early architects of Christian theological thought did not perceive doctrine as a static collection of precepts. Instead, they viewed it as a dynamic and evolving entity, capable of addressing the spiritual and moral needs of an ever-changing community of believers. This perspective was profoundly influenced by a communal understanding of revelation, experienced through both the liturgy and the lived witness of the church.

One cannot underestimate the significance of the Didache or the Shepherd of Hermas in this milieu. These texts were instrumental in laying down foundational teachings, embodying the Spirit-inspired wisdom that was deemed essential for the faithful. The Didache, often referred to as the Teaching of the Twelve Apostles, offered practical guidance on Christian living and church order, while The Shepherd of Hermas provided moral exhortation through allegorical visions. They collectively underscored the importance of maintaining a cohesive communal identity, bound by shared beliefs and practices.

Early Councils like the Council of Jerusalem, held around AD 50, were pioneering in their approach to doctrinal development. Though not as formally structured as later Ecumenical Councils, these gatherings epitomized the nascent church's commitment to addressing theological dilemmas through collective discernment. The Council of Jerusalem, for example, tackled the contentious issue of Gentile conversion and the extent to which Mosaic Law should be applied to new converts. The resolution reached underscored the adaptive and inclusive spirit that would come to characterize Christian doctrinal development.

Moving deeper into the early centuries, testimonies from Church Fathers like Irenaeus and Tertullian expounded on the necessity of holding fast to apostolic teaching while concurrently allowing for the organic maturation of doctrine. Irenaeus, particularly in his seminal work "Against Heresies," argued for the indispensability of Sacred Tradition as a bulwark against heretical interpretations. He saw the continuous guidance of the Holy Spirit as pivotal in revealing the deeper meanings embedded within the apostolic teachings.

Irenaeus' concept of "recapitulation" – the idea that Christ recapitulates in Himself the entire history and future of humanity, thereby perfecting it – was a theological innovation that expanded the horizons of early Christian doctrinal thought. This doctrine encapsulated the belief that every age would bring forth new understandings of the eternal truth, thus supporting the notion that doctrine was not a closed system but an open journey guided by the Spirit.

Tertullian, on the other hand, was instrumental in articulating the necessity of doctrinal unity in the face of growing Montanist influence. His emphasis on the "rule of faith" – a set of core beliefs derived from Scripture and Tradition – highlighted the interdependence of these two sources of divine revelation. Tertullian's juridical mindset brought a certain rigor to theological discussions, ensuring that doctrinal evolution did not deviate from apostolic roots.

As the early church sought to formulate its core beliefs, it contended with multiple external influences, not the least of which were the philosophical traditions of Greco-Roman culture. The interplay between Hellenistic thought and emerging Christian doctrine was complex and profoundly impactful. While some, like Justin Martyr, embraced a synthesis of Christian revelation and Greek philosophy, others remained wary. The resulting doctrinal formulations were thus an intricate tapestry, interwoven with threads of both sacred tradition and reasoned inquiry.

It is worth noting that the development of Christian doctrine was not a linear process but a multifaceted dialogue encompassing divergent views and interpretations. Heresies such as Gnosticism and Arianism emerged as formidable challenges, prompting the church to delineate its teachings more clearly. The need to affirm orthodox beliefs led to the crafting of creeds – concise statements of faith that crystallized core doctrines and provided a unifying framework for the scattered communities of believers.

The Apostles' Creed, for instance, is an early symbol of faith that encapsulated foundational Christian beliefs, serving both as a catechetical tool and a statement of unity. The subsequent Nicene Creed, formulated in the wake of the Council of Nicaea in AD 325, further refined these tenets, addressing Christological controversies that threatened the church's doctrinal integrity. These creeds were not merely doctrinal affirmations but expressions of a living faith, continually informed by and responsive to the Holy Spirit's guidance.

As the church ventured into the Middle Ages, the doctrinal positions established during the early centuries provided a sturdy foundation upon which further theological edifices could be built. The rigorous theological explorations of the Scholastics, the insights of the Church Fathers, and the deliberations of Ecumenical Councils all drew from the rich reservoir of apostolic tradition. This synchronization of past wisdom with present understanding ensured that the development of doctrine remained a dynamic and Spirit-led process.

The trajectory of Christian doctrinal development during the early apostolic era set a compelling precedent for future generations. It demonstrated that while the essence of faith is immutable, the understanding and articulation of that faith must be responsive to the evolving contexts and challenges faced by the church. This early heritage of doctrinal evolution provides a valuable lens through which contemporary theological discourse can contemplate the ongoing journey of faith and understanding within the body of Christ.

In reflecting upon the development of Christian doctrine, it is crucial to recognize that this early period was marked by a profound synthesis of fidelity to received teachings and openness to the Spirit's ongoing revelation. This balance remains essential for any authentic progression in doctrinal understanding. As the church continues its pilgrimage through time, the foundational principles established in the early apostolic church will undoubtedly continue to inform and inspire its pursuit of divine truth.

Chapter 6: Medieval Perspectives on Tradition

In the medieval period, the notion of tradition became a venerable pillar in Catholic theology, owing much to the profound insights of the Scholastics. Thinkers such as Thomas Aquinas endeavored to synthesize reason and faith, illustrating that divine truths handed down through tradition were congruent with rational inquiry. This era saw an unparalleled intertwining of the wisdom of the Church Fathers and the decrees of Ecumenical Councils, offering a unified vision of doctrine that strove to be both comprehensive and exacting. As ecclesiastical authorities wrestled with heresies and divergent interpretations, they leaned heavily on tradition to demarcate orthodoxy from heterodoxy. This reliance was not merely defensive; it was also a creative endeavor that enriched the Church's doctrinal heritage. The medieval synthesis established a theological framework that would become a touchstone for future generations striving to reconcile evolving human understanding with the immutable truths of divine revelation.

Role of the Scholastics

In the vast landscape of medieval theology, the Scholastics played a pivotal role in shaping the understanding of tradition. Their approach was profoundly analytical and systematic, bringing a new dimension to the interpretation of Sacred Scripture and Tradition. The Scholastics aimed to harmonize faith and reason, a task that required deft intellectual prowess and a commitment to the Church's teachings.

Scholasticism emerged in the medieval period as a method of learning rooted in the use of dialectical reasoning. This approach emphasized the rigorous evaluation of arguments, often within the frameworks established by earlier Church Fathers and ecumenical councils. Scholastics meticulously examined theological questions and sought to resolve apparent contradictions in the tradition. Their method was both a continuation and an innovation, preserving the essence of the faith while addressing new intellectual challenges.

Several figures dominated the Scholastic movement, each contributing uniquely to its evolution. Thomas Aquinas, perhaps the most renowned Scholastic, synthesized Aristotelian philosophy with Christian doctrine, providing a comprehensive theological system that remains influential to this day. His "Summa Theologica" is a monumental work that exemplifies the Scholastic method, combining scripture, tradition, and reason in a harmonious triad. By carefully dissecting theological concepts, Aquinas and his contemporaries clarified and expanded the Church's understanding of divine truths.

Another key Scholastic, Anselm of Canterbury, emphasized the concept of "faith seeking understanding." For Anselm, theological inquiry was not merely an academic exercise but a profound spiritual journey. His ontological arguments for the existence of God exemplify the Scholastic commitment to integrating rational examination with deep faith. This delicate balance ensured that the exploration of tradition was not divorced from the lived experience of belief.

The Scholastics also contributed to the development of what became known as the "university system," facilitating an environment where theological and philosophical debates could flourish. These medieval universities became crucibles of intellectual activity, wherein tradition was not only preserved but vigorously examined and, where necessary, rearticulated. The Scholastic method, with its rigorous disputation and emphasis on clarity, set the standard for academic inquiry and influenced not just theology but various branches of knowledge.

Importantly, the Scholastics did not operate in isolation. They engaged deeply with the writings of Church Fathers, such as Augustine and Gregory the Great, to ensure that their innovations were firmly rooted in the established tradition. This engagement demonstrated their respect for the historical continuity of the Church's teachings while also showing their willingness to expand upon them. They saw themselves as stewards of tradition, tasked with its preservation and elucidation for future generations.

The questions tackled by the Scholastics ranged from the nature of the sacraments to the intricacies of the Trinity and the Incarnation. Their work often sought to draw definitive conclusions where the Church's teachings had left room for interpretation. This endeavor, while sometimes controversial, enriched the doctrinal landscape and provided later theologians with robust frameworks to explore new questions and challenges.

One of the lasting impacts of the Scholastic movement is its methodological contribution to the Church's intellectual tradition. The emphasis on dialectic reasoning—where arguments are meticulously analyzed, counterarguments considered, and resolutions formulated—has become a hallmark of Catholic theological scholarship. This method ensures that theological explorations remain disciplined, thorough, and respectful of the complexity of divine truths.

It is also essential to recognize the balance achieved by the Scholastics between innovation and orthodoxy. By rigorously engaging with both reason and revelation, the Scholastics provided a model for how the Church could adapt to new intellectual climates without compromising its core teachings. Their work laid the groundwork for navigating future theological developments and confrontations with emerging philosophical trends.

In the context of medieval perspectives on tradition, the Scholastics show how tradition is not a static inheritance but a dynamic process. They acknowledged that while the truths revealed by God are immutable, the understanding and articulation of these truths can develop over time. This recognition allowed them to address contemporary issues in a manner that was both truthful to the deposit of faith and responsive to new questions.

The legacy of the Scholastics is also seen in the development of Church doctrine. By providing clear and reasoned expositions of complex theological concepts, they facilitated a more profound and accessible understanding of the faith for clergy and laity alike. This doctrinal clarity helped to unify the Church's teachings and provided a bulwark against heretical interpretations that threatened doctrinal integrity.

In conclusion, the role of the Scholastics in the medieval Church's exploration of tradition cannot be overstated. They acted as both guardians and innovators, maintaining the integrity of the Church's teachings while also expanding their understanding through rigorous intellectual inquiry. Their contributions continue to influence Catholic theology, demonstrating the enduring value of their methods and insights. As we reflect on their legacy, it becomes clear that they have bequeathed to the Church not just a body of knowledge but a tradition of seeking understanding through the harmonious interplay of faith and reason.

Influence of Church Fathers and Ecumenical Councils

The medieval period, often seen as the bridge between antiquity and modernity, played a crucial role in the development and preservation of Sacred Tradition within the Catholic Church. The influence of Church Fathers and Ecumenical Councils cannot be overstated as they provided a firm theological foundation and acted as a guiding force in shaping the doctrines and practices that have endured through the ages.

The Church Fathers, those illustrious theological giants whose writings and teachings have become anchors of Christian orthodoxy, exercised profound influence on the medieval understanding of tradition. Figures such as St. Augustine, St. Jerome, and St. Gregory the Great endeavored to elucidate and defend the faith through meticulous exegesis of Scripture, passionate homilies, and extensive theological treatises. Their efforts to collate and interpret the core tenets of Christianity ensured that the tradition was both preserved and transmitted with fidelity.

St. Augustine, often regarded as the doctor of grace, offered a rich and nuanced understanding of tradition. His reflections on grace, original sin, and the nature of the Church not only addressed contemporary heresies like Pelagianism but also laid a theological foundation that would be revisited and expanded by medieval scholastics. Augustine's synthesis of faith and reason became a cornerstone for many medieval theologians who sought to reconcile divine revelation with human understanding.

Similarly, St. Jerome's monumental task of translating the Bible into Latin, known as the Vulgate, provided the Church with an authoritative scriptural text that would be used for centuries. Jerome's scholarship and linguistic acumen ensured that the Scriptures were accessible to the Latin-speaking world, allowing for a more uniform and cohesive transmission of biblical tradition across the Western Church.

Meanwhile, St. Gregory the Great's contributions extended beyond theology into the realm of ecclesiastical administration and pastoral care. Gregory's "Pastoral Rule" and his extensive correspondence offer invaluable insights into the practical application of tradition in the governance of the Church and the spiritual guidance of the laity. His synthesis of monastic wisdom with pastoral duties exemplified a holistic approach to tradition that was both contemplative and active.

In addition to the writings of the Church Fathers, Ecumenical Councils played a pivotal role in defining and defending orthodox tradition. These councils, convened to address urgent theological and ecclesiastical issues, provided a forum for collective discernment and authoritative decision-making. The decrees and canons issued by these councils served as binding declarations that sought to maintain the integrity of the faith amidst various controversies and schisms.

The First Council of Nicaea (325 AD) stands as a testament to the role of ecumenical councils in shaping tradition. Confronted with the Arian controversy, which questioned the divinity of Christ, the council fathers articulated the Nicene Creed, affirming the consubstantiality of the Son with the Father. This creed became a core element of Christian orthodoxy, recited in liturgies and catechesis, thus ensuring the transmission of a unified doctrinal tradition regarding the nature of the Trinity.

Later, the Council of Chalcedon (451 AD) addressed the Christological debates that had arisen from the teachings of Nestorius and Eutyches. The council's definition of the hypostatic union, declaring Christ as fully divine and fully human in one person, provided a critical doctrinal clarification that would shape Christological tradition for centuries. The Chalcedonian Definition served as a benchmark for orthodoxy, guiding theological reflections and ensuring doctrinal continuity within the Church.

The medieval period also witnessed the influence of subsequent councils, such as the Second Council of Nicaea (787 AD), which addressed the iconoclastic controversy. The council's affirmation of the veneration of icons underscored the importance of sacred images in Christian worship and devotion, thereby solidifying a tradition that recognized the incarnational reality of the Christian faith. By affirming the legitimacy of icons, the council preserved a vital aspect of liturgical and spiritual tradition that continues to resonate within the Church.

Moreover, the medieval synthesis of tradition benefitted from the integration of Patristic wisdom with the emerging scholastic methodology. The scholastics, building upon the foundations laid by the Church Fathers and the councils, employed rigorous dialectical reasoning to explore and systematize theological truths. Figures such as Anselm of Canterbury and Thomas Aquinas expanded upon the Patristic legacy by engaging with philosophical concepts and crafting comprehensive theological systems that sought to harmonize faith with reason.

Thomas Aquinas, in particular, drew extensively from Augustine and the ecumenical councils, weaving their teachings into his Summa Theologica. Aquinas' synthesis of Aristotelian philosophy with Christian theology provided a robust intellectual framework that addressed both theological and philosophical inquiries. His methodical approach to tradition, characterized by precise definitions and logical arguments, played a significant role in the development of Catholic doctrine and continues to be a reference point for contemporary theologians.

Furthermore, the medieval period saw the establishment of canonical collections, which systematically organized the decrees of councils and the writings of the Church Fathers. These collections, such as Gratian's Decretum, served as indispensable compendiums of ecclesiastical law and doctrine, aiding in the uniform application of tradition across Christendom. The codification of these texts ensured that the wisdom of the Church Fathers and the decisions of the councils remained accessible to future generations, thereby facilitating the preservation and transmission of tradition.

In summary, the influence of the Church Fathers and Ecumenical Councils on medieval perspectives of tradition cannot be overstated. The writings and teachings of the Church Fathers provided a rich reservoir of theological insights that shaped the medieval understanding of the faith, while the ecumenical councils offered authoritative declarations that safeguarded doctrinal integrity. Together, these sources of tradition formed a cohesive and dynamic foundation that enabled the Church to navigate the complexities of the medieval period and continue its mission of transmitting the immutable and eternal revealed truths from God through His bride, the Church.

Chapter 7: Reformation and Counter-Reformation Views

The Reformation and Counter-Reformation represent pivotal epochs in the theological and ecclesiastical annals of the Church, characterized by fervent confrontations and profound reaffirmations. Protestant Reformers, spearheaded by figures like Martin Luther and John Calvin, launched formidable challenges to Catholic Tradition, scrutinizing its scriptural underpinnings and condemning perceived excesses and corruptions. This provoked the Church to an august and resolute response through the Council of Trent, a seminal gathering that not only countered Protestant critiques but also crystallized the Church's doctrines on Tradition. The Council's decrees underscored the symbiotic relationship between Scripture and Tradition, reaffirming their co-equal authority in divine revelation. Hence, this era witnessed a dialectic of discord and consolidation, shaping the contours of Catholic theology in ways that continue to resonate through centuries of ecclesial discourse.

Protestant Challenges to Catholic Tradition

Dissenters such as Martin Luther and John Calvin ignited the Protestant Reformation, primarily targeting what they perceived as the Roman Catholic Church's over-reliance on tradition at the expense of scriptural authority. Luther's clarion call for "sola scriptura" — by scripture alone — posited that the Bible is the sole infallible source of authority for Christian faith and practice. The principle of "sola scriptura" was a direct challenge to the Catholic integration of Sacred Tradition and Sacred Scripture as twin pillars of divine revelation. By advocating "sola scriptura," Protestant reformers sought to strip away layers of tradition and focus solely on the earliest biblical texts, contending that tradition had accumulated extraneous rituals and doctrines over the centuries.

One of the significant points of contention was the role of the Church's Magisterium, or teaching authority. The Catholic Church upheld that the Pope and ecumenical councils had been endowed with the Holy Spirit's guidance to interpret both Scripture and Tradition authoritatively. Protestants, however, argued that this led to human additions which distorted the original Gospel message. Such as the selling of indulgences and the veneration of saints and relics were deemed examples of how tradition had gone astray. Primitive Christianity, they argued, was far simpler and purer, unencumbered by what they considered the accretions of tradition.

Calvin's arguments went further to contest the Catholic view of the sacraments. While Catholicism held to seven sacraments, believing them to be instituted by Christ and necessary for salvation, Protestant reformers generally accepted only two — baptism and the Eucharist — which they argued were explicitly ordained by Christ in the New Testament. This doctrinal rift highlighted deeper theological differences about how Sacred Tradition informed sacramental theology. For Catholics, Tradition revealed the full understanding and proper administration of the sacraments, an idea firmly rejected by the reformers who saw it as a deviation from Scripture.

The development of Marian doctrines serves as another profound example of Protestant challenges to Catholic tradition. Over centuries, the Catholic Church developed a rich tradition of Marian theology, encompassing doctrines like the Immaculate Conception and the Assumption. Protestants largely rejected these, arguing they lacked explicit biblical support. The Protestant perspective saw these doctrines as symptomatic of a broader trend where Tradition had excessively supplemented or even eclipsed Scriptural revelation.

In response to Protestant critiques, the Catholic Church convened the Council of Trent (1545-1563), which robustly affirmed the interwoven nature of Scripture and Tradition. The Council declared that both Scripture and Tradition are received with equal sentiments of devotion and reverence. This was seen as a necessary bulwark against what the Church perceived as the fragmentation and subjectivity inherent in "sola scriptura". By doing so, it sought to anchor the faith in the apostolic teachings and lived experience passed down through the ages, arguing that the Bible itself emerged from the Church's tradition.

Trent also emphasized the role of the Magisterium in correctly interpreting scripture and tradition, thus reinforcing the Church's teaching authority. In the face of Protestant assertions that individual believers could discern biblical truths on their own, the Council stressed the risk of misinterpretation and doctrinal chaos. According to Catholic teaching, the Holy Spirit's guidance was not given to individual interpretations but to the Church collectively through its leaders.

Moreover, Protestant iconoclasm — the destruction of religious images — drew sharp lines between Protestant and Catholic practice. Reformers condemned what they saw as idolatry in the veneration of icons, statues, and relics, rooted in Catholic tradition. By contrast, the Catholic Church saw these as legitimate expressions of piety that connected believers with the holy. The divergence on this issue was emblematic of broader theological discrepancies about how visible symbols and traditions mediated divine realities.

A nuanced issue was the understanding of justification and salvation. Martin Luther famously declared that humans are justified by faith alone ("sola fide"), not by works, challenging a Catholic theology that integrated both faith and works within the framework of grace. This radically challenged Catholic understandings of Tradition's role in moral teaching and spiritual life, where works were seen as essential manifestations of God's grace rather than simply evidence of faith.

The engagement between Protestantism and Catholicism during the Reformation ultimately spurred both theological traditions to refine and clarify their teachings. Protestant challenges prompted Catholics to articulate more clearly the basis of their traditions, leading to deeper intellectual rigor and reflection on the foundational role of Tradition in the life of the Church. This period was not merely one of entrenchment but also of profound theological development and dialogue, laying the groundwork for future ecumenical endeavors.

In summary, Protestant challenges to Catholic tradition were multifaceted, targeting doctrinal teachings, ecclesiastical authority, sacramental theology, and devotional practices. The Reformation was a catalyst that forced the Catholic Church to defend and articulate its understanding of the inseparability of Sacred Tradition and Sacred Scripture. This contentious interaction shaped both theological landscapes, fostering a dynamic interplay that continues to influence Christian thought today. As the Church engaged with these challenges, it deepened its commitment to the traditions viewed not as mere human constructs but as integral to the faith transmitted from the apostles.

Council of Trent and the Affirmation of Tradition

The Council of Trent, convened between 1545 and 1563, emerged as a pivotal moment in the history of Catholicism, especially concerning the affirmation and crystallization of Sacred Tradition. During this period of intense theological upheaval sparked by the Protestant Reformation, the Catholic Church faced formidable challenges to its doctrines and practices. The Council of Trent not only served as a counter-reformation measure but also as a profound affirmation of the integral role that Tradition plays in Catholic theology.

The Council's response to the Reformers' critiques was anything but superficial. By thoroughly reevaluating and subsequently affirming its doctrines, the Catholic Church underscored the importance of Tradition as complementary to Sacred Scripture. This idea was not novel, having roots in the teachings of early church fathers and councils. Still, the urgency of the Reformation necessitated a more explicit and formal delineation of these beliefs.

One key decision of the Council of Trent was its unequivocal assertion that both Scripture and Tradition are essential for a full comprehension of divine revelation. The Protestant Reformation had elevated Scripture—sola scriptura—as the sole source of divine authority. In stark contrast, the Council of Trent declared that the written word and unwritten traditions, transmitted through the Apostles under the guidance of the Holy Spirit, are both indispensable.

Furthermore, Trent provided clear definitions and dogmas that would guide the faithful and future generations. Among its various decrees, the Council emphasized the divine inspiration and canonical status of the deuterocanonical books, which had been contested by Protestant reformers. This reinforcement of the canon showcases how deeply the Church valued Tradition, as it harkens back to the Septuagint, the Greek translation of Hebrew Scriptures used by early Christians.

The Council also addressed the interpretation of Scripture, affirming the Church's authority to offer authentic interpretations. This was a direct response to the multiplicity of interpretations emerging from Protestant circles, which threatened ecclesial unity. By safeguarding the interpretative power of the Magisterium, the Council cemented the idea that Tradition serves as a living conduit for understanding Scripture.

Moreover, the sacraments received attention, with Trent codifying their number at seven and elaborating on their efficacy stemming not from the dispositions of the minister but from the actions of Christ himself, enacted through the Church. This stood in direct opposition to various Reformation claims that diminished or denied the sacramental system upheld by Catholic Tradition.

In addition to theological affirmations, the Council of Trent initiated significant reforms within the Church's administrative and pastoral practices. One of the most notable outcomes was the establishment of seminaries for the proper training of clergy. This was not merely an educational reform; it was an effort to ensure that those responsible for teaching Tradition and performing sacramental rites were themselves deeply rooted in both Scripture and Tradition.

Furthermore, the Council's reforms had a considerable impact on liturgical practices, including the standardization of the Mass. The promulgation of the Roman Missal by Pope Pius V in 1570 aimed to preserve liturgical unity and underscore the continuity of Tradition in worship. This had the effect of ensuring that the faithful across different regions experienced a unified form of liturgical expression, thereby reinforcing the collective identity of the Church through shared tradition.

From the vantage point of ecclesiology, the Council of Trent solidified the connection between Tradition and the Church's teaching authority. The decrees articulated during the sessions of the Council made it clear that the bishops, in communion with the Pope, served as guardians of both Scripture and Tradition. This ecclesiological stance was crucial for maintaining doctrinal continuity and protecting the Church from what it saw as the fragmented doctrinal landscape created by the Reformation.

In examining the broader impact of the Council, one cannot overlook the spiritual and psychological reassurance it provided to the faithful. By reaffirming core doctrines and establishing clear guidelines, the Council of Trent offered stability and a reaffirmed sense of purpose to a community beset by doubt and discord. This point is often underscored by historians who note the revitalizing effect Trent had on Catholic spirituality and religious practice.

The Council's legacy extends beyond mere doctrinal affirmations and institutional reforms; it embodied a resilient reaffirmation of the Church's mission. By unambiguously asserting the coequal importance of Scripture and Tradition, the Council of Trent crystallized a theological framework that has endured for centuries. This enduring legacy resonates to this day, illustrating how deeply entrenched and dynamic the concept of Tradition is within Catholicism.

In conclusion, the Council of Trent's affirmation of Tradition was not just a reactionary countermeasure to the Protestant Reformation but a profound rearticulation of a foundational aspect of Catholic theology. It highlighted the Church's commitment to preserving and transmitting immutable truths through both Scripture and the lived experience of the faith community—ensuring that, despite temporal challenges, the eternal wisdom of the Church remains accessible and comprehensible to all who seek it.

Chapter 8: Modern Developments in Understanding Tradition

As we transition into modernity, the understanding of Sacred Tradition has undergone significant transformations, profoundly influenced by the Enlightenment and the modern theological environment. With the dawn of rational inquiry and historical criticism, longstanding beliefs faced scrutiny, compelling theologians to revisit and reinterpret traditional tenets. The Second Vatican Council (Vatican II) marked a watershed moment, embracing a renewed orthodoxy that sought to make Tradition more accessible and relevant in a rapidly changing world. Far from discarding the past, this era built upon it, infusing ancient truths with contemporary insights to address the spiritual and intellectual needs of today's faithful. Consequently, the convergence of historical consciousness and doctrinal continuity has reanimated Catholic Tradition, ensuring its robust presence in modern theological discourse. The ongoing dialogue between fidelity to the roots and the demands of modernity remains one of the most dynamic aspects of contemporary Catholicism.

Impact of the Enlightenment and Modernity

The Enlightenment, a period of profound intellectual and philosophical transformation, fundamentally reshaped society's views on many long-held traditions, including those of Roman Catholicism. Emerging in the 17th and 18th centuries, this movement championed ideas such as reason, individualism, and skepticism of authority, which directly challenged the notion of Sacred Tradition in the Catholic Church. Rational discourse and empirical evidence became the hallmarks of truth, often relegating faith and ecclesiastical tradition to the periphery.

This era saw the waning influence of ecclesiastical authority as the primary arbiter of truth, replaced by a growing reliance on scientific understanding and reasoned debate. The Enlightenment's emphasis on autonomous human reasoning posed a formidable challenge to the Catholic understanding of Tradition, which hinges on the continuity and communal discernment of revealed truths. Consequently, theologians and church authorities found themselves tasked with defending the relevance and authenticity of Sacred Tradition within an increasingly secular and rational world.

Ironically, the Enlightenment, while skeptical of tradition, also inadvertently forced the Church to refine and articulate the essentials of what constitutes Catholic Tradition. This period marked a pivotal point where the Church sought to define Sacred Tradition not merely as an antiquated accumulation of customs but as a living transmission of faith, intertwined with Sacred Scripture and the teachings of the Magisterium. The Enlightenment's critique helped prompt the Church to clarify that Tradition was dynamic rather than static, capable of engaging the intellectual currents of the time.

Fast forward to the dawn of Modernity in the 19th and 20th centuries, another significant challenge arose with the advent of modern science, historical-critical methods, and rapidly changing social norms. Modernity brought advancements in technology and communication, thrusting society into an era of connectivity and accelerated change. These developments further tested the Church's ability to present Tradition as a beacon of eternal truths in a world increasingly infatuated with progress and novelty.

A notable feature of this epoch was the rise of historical-critical methods in biblical scholarship. These scholarly approaches scrutinized the historical contexts and literary compositions of Scripture, leading to new interpretations that sometimes conflicted with traditional views. Catholic scholars had to navigate these waters carefully, ensuring that such methods could be employed to deepen understanding without undermining the core tenets of faith. The Church's gradual acceptance and adaptation of these methods signaled an openness to engage with contemporary intellectual tools while safeguarding the integral aspects of faith and Tradition.

Moreover, the encyclicals and doctrinal pronouncements during this period reflect an ongoing effort to reconcile the immutable truths of the faith with contemporary insights. Documents from Popes such as Leo XIII and Pius XII, among others, sought to address the pressing questions posed by modern science and philosophy. Encyclicals like "Providentissimus Deus" and "Divino Afflante Spiritu" encouraged the faithful to read Scriptures not merely in a literal sense but with an awareness of historical and literary contexts, showcasing the Church's adaptability in embracing scholarly advancements without compromising the essence of Tradition.

The Second Vatican Council (1962-1965) represents perhaps the most significant modern development in understanding Tradition in light of Enlightenment and Modernity influences. Vatican II aimed to address the role of the Church in a changing world and sought to present Tradition and doctrine in ways that resonated with contemporary human experiences and intellectual pursuits. Documents such as "Dei Verbum" emphatically state that both Scripture and Tradition must be accepted and honored with equal sentiments of devotion and reverence, underscoring their interdependent relationship within the revelation.

Vatican II did not shy away from engaging with the modern world; rather, it sought to reinterpret Tradition in light of contemporary realities. This engagement meant affirming the timeless nature of core doctrinal truths while recognizing the pastoral need to address modern existential questions. This dual approach ensured that Tradition remained a living, fluid conduit of divine truth, readily accessible and relevant to the faithful.

The theological and pastoral challenges experienced by the Church in reconciling Tradition with Enlightenment and Modernity also led to significant internal debates and developments. On one hand, theologians like Yves Congar advocated for an aggiornamento—a bringing up to date—of Church teachings and practices, emphasizing that Tradition was not an immovable object but rather a dynamic process guided by the Holy Spirit. On the other hand, more conservative voices expressed concerns over diluting or compromising essential elements of the faith in an overly accommodating response to modernity.

These internal debates highlighted the delicate balance the Church strived to maintain: preserving the purity and continuity of Sacred Tradition while remaining pastorally sensitive and intellectually engaged with an evolving world. This balancing act continues to be a central theme in contemporary theological discourse, reflecting the enduring impact of Enlightenment and Modernity on the Church's self-understanding and its articulation of Tradition.

In conclusion, the Enlightenment and Modernity catalyzed a profound introspection within the Roman Catholic Church about the nature and relevance of Sacred Tradition. These epochs compelled the Church to demonstrate that Tradition is neither an archaic relic nor antithetical to reason and progress. Instead, it is a living heritage, enriched by its encounter with reason, evolving with time, yet steadfast in its essence. Such a dynamic and resilient understanding of Tradition ensures that the divine truths entrusted to the Church continue to guide humanity amid the ceaseless currents of change and progress.

Vatican II and Contemporary Views

One cannot speak of modern developments in understanding tradition without addressing the Second Vatican Council, commonly referred to as Vatican II. Convened by Pope John XXIII and occurring from 1962 to 1965, Vatican II sought, among other things, to address and clarify the Catholic Church's position on Sacred Tradition in the context of a rapidly changing world. This ecumenical council produced numerous documents, with "Dei Verbum," the "Dogmatic Constitution on Divine Revelation," being particularly pivotal for our discussion.

"Dei Verbum" significantly reshaped theological perspectives on tradition by emphasizing the interconnectedness between Sacred Scripture and Sacred Tradition. The document underscored that both are essential for the transmission of divine revelation, arguing against the notion that one stands superior to the other. It stated, "Sacred Tradition and Sacred Scripture form one sacred deposit of the word of God," a profound assertion that intended to harmonize these two pillars of the faith. This represents a nuanced yet critical shift from previous understandings, where tradition was sometimes envisioned as an ancillary appendage to Scripture.

The council made it clear that the living tradition of the Church is dynamic and continues to grow through the centuries. It acknowledged the role of the Holy Spirit in guiding the Church's Magisterium, the teaching authority, to faithfully interpret and transmit the teachings of Christ and the Apostles. Importantly, it emphasized that this process is not static; it involves discernment, prayer, and a deep engagement with the signs of the times. Through this lens, tradition is not merely a relic of the past but is alive and responsive to contemporary contexts.

Vatican II also brought forth a greater participatory role for the laity in the life of the Church, redefining the relationship between the hierarchy and the faithful. This had implications for how tradition was received and experienced by the broader community. The Council's inclusive tone enabled a more democratized understanding of tradition, encouraging lay

Catholics to delve into scripture and theology, thereby diversifying the voices contributing to the understanding and application of tradition.

Moreover, the Council encouraged an aggiornamento—a bringing up to date—that sought to engage modernity rather than oppose it. This ethos permeated its approach to tradition, suggesting that understanding the faith must be continually updated to address contemporary issues and insights. However, this approach also generated various interpretations and reactions, sometimes causing friction between progressives and conservatives within the Church.

Contemporary theological debates continue to revolve around the interpretations of Vatican II's teachings. Some theologians, inspired by the Council's spirit, advocate for further reforms that they believe are in keeping with the Conciliar vision. They argue for an ever-progressive understanding of tradition that integrates advancements in human knowledge, ethical considerations, and social justice. These theologians stress the need for dialogue between tradition and contemporary human experiences, holding that tradition, while rooted in the past, must speak meaningfully to the present.

On the other hand, there are those who caution against what they perceive as the overextension of the Council's reforms. They argue that too much innovation runs the risk of diluting core doctrinal truths. These theologians emphasize a hermeneutic of continuity, asserting that the development of tradition should always remain faithfully aligned with the historical teachings of the Church. This perspective stresses caution and deliberate pacing in interpreting Vatican II's documents, emphasizing fidelity over innovation.

One must also consider the global and cultural dimensions that Vatican II touched upon. The Council's universal outlook encouraged local cultures to express the faith within their own linguistic, social, and cultural contexts. This inculturation was a significant departure from the previously more Eurocentric expression of Catholicism. By promoting this diversity, Vatican II recognized that while the essence of tradition is universal, its expression need not be uniform.

Another contemporary view pertains to the role of ecumenism as encouraged by Vatican II. The Council marked a significant shift towards engaging with other Christian denominations and even non-Christian faiths, fostering a spirit of dialogue rather than confrontation. This ecumenical approach has opened avenues for understanding tradition not just as a boundary marker of Catholic identity but as a bridge for mutual enrichment and unity among diverse Christian traditions and beyond.

The hermeneutics of Vatican II, therefore, offer a rich and complex terrain for the contemporary Church as it seeks to navigate the challenges and opportunities of the present age. The Council's documents left ample room for interpretation, which has led to both unity and division within the Church. This ongoing interpretative process is, in itself, a testament to the living nature of Sacred Tradition—a tradition that, while rooted in core, immutable truths, continues to grow and respond to the exigencies of human existence.

It becomes evident that Vatican II remains a pivotal point for contemporary views on tradition. Its call to engage modernity with discernment while remaining faithful to the essence of the Church's teachings encapsulates the dynamic tension within which tradition operates. As theologians, scholars, Roman Catholics, historians, and philosophers continue to delve into these issues, they contribute to the ongoing story of Sacred Tradition, one that is perpetually unfolding yet steadfastly anchored in its divine origin. The challenge lies in maintaining this balance, ensuring that the dynamic nature of tradition does not lose sight of its eternal truths while striving to be ever-relevant in a changing world.

Chapter 9: Tradition in Catholic Doctrine and Practice

Tradition in Catholic doctrine and practice holds a central role, intertwining with the Church's liturgical and sacramental life, and shaping its theological landscape through the guiding authority of the Magisterium. Across the centuries, liturgical practices—from the Eucharist to the rites of baptism and confirmation—have been meticulously preserved and transmitted, embodying the living faith of the Church. Sacramental theology, rooted in these ancient traditions, serves as a tangible means through which believers encounter divine grace, reflecting the unchanging truths of faith. The Magisterium, vested with the responsibility of authentically interpreting the Word of God, upholds and expounds tradition with a fidelity that ensures continuity and unity within the Church. This dynamic interplay of tradition, liturgy, and teaching authority forms the bedrock of Catholic identity, illuminating the pathway for believers striving to comprehend and live out the eternal and immutable truths handed down through generations.

Liturgical Practices and Sacramental Theology

The liturgies of the Catholic Church are a visible enactment of the invisible mysteries of God's grace, rooted in both Sacred Scripture and Sacred Tradition. These liturgical practices are not mere formalities but sacramental expressions through which divine grace is mediated to the faithful. The liturgical year, sacraments, and the liturgy of the hours are foundational components of Catholic worship, each elucidating an aspect of the Christian journey from birth to eternal life.

At the heart of Catholic liturgical practices lies the Eucharist, also called the "source and summit" of Christian life. The celebration of the Eucharist commemorates the Last Supper, the Passion, and the Resurrection of Christ. This sacrament embodies profound theological significance—it is a memorial of Jesus' sacrifice and a means of communion with God. The doctrine of Transubstantiation, defined at the Council of Trent, asserts that the bread and wine become the true Body and Blood of Christ. This transformation anchors the faithful in a tactile experience of divine mystery.

Each sacrament holds a specific place within the theological framework of the Church. Baptism, the gateway sacrament, initiates individuals into the Body of Christ. It not only cleanses from original sin but also imparts sanctifying grace, making one a new creation in Christ. Confirmation, often administered by a bishop, confers the gifts of the Holy Spirit, empowering the faithful to live out their Christian vocation more fully.

Despite their theological significance, the sacraments are also highly ritualistic. Their performance is governed by specific rubrics detailed in liturgical books. The rites of each sacrament comprise prayers, readings from Scripture, and symbolic acts like the laying on of hands, anointing with oil, and the use of sacramental signs (e.g., water, bread, and wine). These elements collectively constitute the rich tapestry of Catholic worship, a tradition that has evolved through the centuries while retaining its core essence.

The sacrament of Penance or Reconciliation, often misunderstood, is another pillar of Catholic sacramental theology. Rooted in Jesus' command to forgive sins, it offers a channel for the faithful to receive absolution from sin through the ministry of a priest. This sacrament is a testimony to God's infinite mercy and invites the penitent to a profound conversion of heart. Its importance was re-emphasized during the Counter-Reformation as a response to Protestant critiques.

Matrimony and Holy Orders deserve special mention as they are sacraments of service. In marriage, a man and woman are consecrated to each other in a lifelong covenant, mirroring the unbreakable bond between Christ and His Church. Holy Orders, on the other hand, configures recipients into Christ's priesthood through the threefold ministry of deacon, priest, and bishop. These sacraments deepen our understanding of relational and communal aspects of divine grace.

Liturgical practices and the theology underpinning them are inseparable from the Magisterium's teachings. The Magisterium, comprising the Pope and the bishops, serves as the Church's authentic teaching authority. Their pronouncements on liturgical worship and sacramental theology carry weight, ensuring fidelity to apostolic tradition. Enhancements in liturgical documents, such as the Roman Missal, signify a continuing engagement with the perennial truths of the faith.

The Liturgy of the Hours, or the Divine Office, offers another dimension to Catholic worship. Rooted in ancient Jewish prayer traditions, this series of daily prayers sanctifies the hours of the day. Through psalms, canticles, and readings, the faithful participate in the eternal liturgy of heaven, echoing the ceaseless praise offered by the angels and saints. It provides a rhythm to spiritual life, interweaving ordinary time with moments of divine encounter.

Vatican II brought significant reforms to liturgical practices, advocating for active participation of the laity and allowing the use of vernacular languages in the Mass. These changes were not merely cosmetic; they aimed to deepen the faithful's engagement with the sacred mysteries. By opening up the liturgy, the Church sought to fulfill its mission of evangelization more effectively, bridging the gap between tradition and contemporary experience.

One cannot overlook the sacramentals in discussing Catholic liturgical practices. Unlike sacraments, sacramentals are sacred signs instituted by the Church to signify spiritual effects obtained through the Church's intercession. These include blessings, consecrations, and exorcisms. While not conferring grace in the way sacraments do, they prepare individuals to receive grace and dispose them favorably towards cooperation with it.

Understanding the Church's liturgical and sacramental practices necessitates a dive into the theological underpinnings that sustain them. It is not hyperbolic to state that these practices are a living tradition, embodied and enacted in the quotidian lives of the faithful. Each gesture, word, and symbol embedded in the liturgy serves to bring the divine into the temporal realm, to make the invisible visible.

This framework of liturgical and sacramental theology is a testament to how doctrine and practice are interwoven. Through the centuries, Church Fathers, scholastics, and modern theologians have grappled with articulating these mysteries in ways that are both faithful to tradition and resonant with contemporary needs. Their contributions enrich the ongoing dialogue about how best to embody the faith in worship and sacrament.

The Church's rich liturgical calendar provides a structured approach to celebrating the mysteries of Christ's life, death, resurrection, and glorification. Seasons like Advent, Lent, and Easter are not mere commemorations but participatory experiences inviting the faithful into the redemptive narrative. Each season and feast day offers unique insights into the inexhaustible mystery of God's salvific plan.

In sum, Catholic liturgical practices and sacramental theology are deeply interwoven elements of a vibrant tradition, continually renewed yet firmly rooted in apostolic teachings. By exploring these practices, one gains profound insights into the Church's mission to sanctify time, space, and human existence itself through the divine grace that flows from Christ and His Church.

Role of the Magisterium

The Magisterium, the teaching authority of the Roman Catholic Church, plays an integral role in interpreting and preserving Sacred Tradition. Entrusted primarily to the Pope and the bishops in communion with him, the Magisterium ensures that the truths of faith are authentically transmitted across generations. This responsibility encompasses more than just doctrinal pronouncements; it includes safeguarding the Church's liturgical practices and moral teachings. The Magisterium functions as a living voice, dynamically interacting with the Deposit of Faith — a term encompassing both Sacred Scripture and Sacred Tradition.

Throughout history, the role of the Magisterium has been pivotal in addressing theological controversies and safeguarding orthodoxy. For instance, during the early ecumenical councils, such as Nicaea and Chalcedon, the Magisterium was instrumental in clarifying doctrines about the nature of Christ and the Holy Trinity. These councils were not merely about settling theological disputes but about preserving the integrity of the faith handed down through the apostles. The decisions made in these councils, guided by the Magisterium, continue to influence Catholic doctrine today.

In a broader sense, the Magisterium also serves a pastoral role. It guides the faithful in understanding complex theological issues and in applying them to everyday life. This guidance is seen in papal encyclicals, pastoral letters, and other ecclesiastical documents that address contemporary moral and social issues. While the content and context may change over time, the fundamental truths remain consistent, demonstrating the Church's commitment to an immutable faith amidst a changing world.

This dual role of preserving doctrinal purity and providing pastoral guidance is evident in how the Church responds to new challenges. For instance, the Second Vatican Council (Vatican II), convened by Pope John XXIII, exemplified the Magisterium's role in addressing modernity. The council sought to engage the modern world without compromising the core tenets of the faith, resulting in documents that rejuvenated liturgical practices and promoted a deeper understanding of the Church's mission.

Moreover, the Magisterium operates within a framework that balances tradition with a living, dynamic faith. It is not an authoritarian imposition but rather a custodianship that invites participation from the community of believers. Lay theologians, clergy, and even ecumenical dialogues contribute to the Magisterium's work. This collaborative approach ensures that the teachings remain relevant, providing a bridge between the ancient faith and contemporary understanding.

One of the key functions of the Magisterium is the interpretation of Sacred Scripture. Guided by the Holy Spirit, it provides the authoritative interpretation that maintains the coherence of the Church's teachings. For example, the Catechism of the Catholic Church, a comprehensive summary of doctrine, embodies the collaborative and interpretative work of the Magisterium. It serves as a reference point for understanding the faith, integrating both Scripture and Tradition in a cohesive manner.

In discussing the role of the Magisterium, it's essential to consider its infallibility on matters of faith and morals when pronounced ex cathedra by the Pope. This concept, while often misunderstood, underscores the Church's belief in divine guidance in preserving the truth. The doctrine of infallibility, defined during the First Vatican Council in 1870, assures the faithful that certain declarations made by the Pope are free from error. This infallibility is not a personal attribute of the Pope but a gift to the Church, rooted in the promise of Christ to Peter and his successors.

The Magisterium's role extends to its interaction with Sacred Tradition, which is not static but living. Tradition, as understood by the Church, is the dynamic transmission of the faith through generations, encompassing teachings, liturgy, Church Fathers' writings, and ecumenical councils' decrees. The Magisterium serves as the interpreter and guardian of this Tradition, ensuring that it remains faithful to the apostolic witness while engaging with contemporary issues.

Thus, the Magisterium stands as the Church's custodian of truth, a role it fulfills through various means. Councils, such as Trent and Vatican II, have been instrumental in defining and clarifying doctrinal matters. Encyclicals, bullae, and other papal documents provide guidance on pressing moral and social issues. Bishops, in communion with the Pope, ensure that the teachings are appropriately disseminated at the diocesan level.

Additionally, the Magisterium addresses the development of doctrine, recognizing that while doctrines are immutable in their essence, their understanding and articulation can grow. This development does not signify a change in truths but a deeper understanding, as guided by the Holy Spirit. A prime example is the doctrine of the Immaculate Conception, which, although rooted in early Church teachings, was infallibly defined by Pope Pius IX in 1854 in the apostolic constitution *Ineffabilis Deus* after centuries of theological reflection.

The Magisterium also navigates complex ethical issues by providing moral guidance that aligns with the Church's teachings. In recent times, this has included positions on bioethics, social justice, and human dignity. Encyclicals such as *Laudato Si'* and *Evangelium Vitae* exemplify the Magisterium's response to contemporary challenges, emphasizing respect for creation and the sanctity of life, respectively.

In summary, the Magisterium is central to the life of the Roman Catholic Church. It acts as both guardian and interpreter of Sacred Tradition and Scripture, ensuring that the faith remains true to the apostolic witness. Through councils, teachings, and pastoral guidance, the Magisterium navigates the complexities of each age, offering the faithful direction and assurance. It underscores the belief that the Church, as the Bride of Christ, is led by the Holy Spirit in all truth, preserving the deposit of faith through the centuries.

Chapter 10: Tradition and Ecumenism

Engaging with the broader Christian community, Catholic theology faces the complex yet invigorating task of bridging doctrinal divides through the lens of Tradition. This chapter delves into how centuries-old beliefs and practices, held sacred by the Roman Catholic Church, find common ground or contention in inter-denominational dialogues. Tradition here is not just a static repository of ancient wisdom, but a dynamic instrument in fostering ecumenical relationships. Through thoughtful negotiation and mutual respect, Tradition opens a pathway for incorporating diverse theological perspectives, enabling a deeper, more inclusive expression of the Christian faith. This dialogical process underscores the significance of shared reverence for historical continuity while addressing modern challenges to unity. As Catholic theologians navigate these intricate waters, they must balance preserving the integrity of their own Tradition with fostering genuine, meaningful connections with other faith communities.

Dialogue with Other Christian Denominations

The dialogue between Roman Catholicism and other Christian denominations is a complex and multifaceted endeavor, deeply rooted in the shared yet divergent histories that have shaped various Christian traditions over the centuries. This conversation is not merely an academic or theological exercise but a living and dynamic process that holds profound implications for the unity of the Christian Church as a whole. It demands a nuanced understanding of the historical and theological contexts that have led to both commonalities and differences among the various branches of Christianity.

Engagement with other Christian denominations often begins with recognizing the shared foundations present in the early Church and the Apostolic Tradition. Despite the divisions that emerged post-Reformation, the Catholic Church has consistently sought avenues for reconciliation and mutual understanding, emphasizing the importance of dialogue in the spirit of ecumenism. The Second Vatican Council marked a significant shift in this regard, opening new doors for conversation and collaboration that had been largely shut for centuries.

One of the central tenets of ecumenical dialogue is the acknowledgment of Sacred Tradition as a formative element of Christian identity, beyond just the confines of Scripture. While the Catholic Church maintains that Sacred Tradition encompasses the fullness of divine revelation transmitted through the Apostles and preserved by the Church's Magisterium, it also recognizes that other Christian communities have developed their own understandings and interpretations of this Tradition.

Ecumenical efforts are often characterized by attempts to bridge doctrinal divides, particularly concerning issues such as the sacraments, ecclesiology, and authority. The Catholic Church has approached these dialogues through various bilateral and multilateral commissions, fostering discussions with Orthodox, Protestant, and Anglican communities. These dialogues have sometimes resulted in significant agreements, like the Joint Declaration on the Doctrine of Justification with the Lutheran World Federation, demonstrating the potential for common ground even in areas of deep-seated theological contention.

Moreover, the role of Tradition in maintaining the continuity and coherence of the Christian faith is a point of both convergence and divergence among denominations. For instance, the Orthodox Churches share a considerable overlap with Catholic understandings of Tradition, emphasizing the role of the Church Fathers and Ecumenical Councils. However, the Orthodox tradition places a distinct emphasis on the living experience of the Holy Spirit within the ecclesial community, occasionally leading to different doctrinal emphases and liturgical practices.

Conversely, Protestant denominations, particularly those stemming from the Reformation, often prioritize the authority of Scripture over Tradition. This sola scriptura principle has been a significant source of contention but also a starting point for rich and meaningful dialogue. Addressing this requires a careful exploration of how Tradition and Scripture function together as dual authorities in Catholic theology, as opposed to the more Scripture-centric focus of many Protestant traditions.

In these dialogues, it is essential to appreciate the historical contexts out of which different theological positions emerged. Many Protestant critiques of Catholic Tradition arose out of a reaction against perceived abuses and excesses in the medieval Church – issues that have been ameliorated to varying extents by modern reforms within Catholicism. Understanding these historical dynamics helps to frame current discussions in a more empathetic and constructive light.

Additionally, dialogues often involve addressing practical expressions of faith that reveal underlying theological principles. For example, the role of the liturgy, the sacraments, and ecclesial authority are not just abstract theological concepts but are lived realities that shape the faith and practice of Christian communities. Here, ecumenical dialogue seeks to find a delicate balance between genuine respect for diversity and a commitment to the unity that Christ himself prayed for.

Another critical aspect of these conversations is the role of the Magisterium in interpreting and preserving Tradition. The Catholic

Church views the Magisterium – the teaching authority vested in the Pope and bishops – as an essential guardian of the faith, ensuring the correct transmission of divine revelation. This concept often contrasts with more decentralized Protestant ecclesial structures, which may rely on a broader interpretative community or individual conscience in matters of doctrine.

The dialogue with the Anglican Communion is noteworthy for its unique historical and theological dimensions. The Anglican tradition, with its blend of catholic and reformed elements, offers fertile ground for ecumenical conversations. Initiatives such as the Anglican-Roman Catholic International Commission (ARCIC) have produced significant documents on topics like authority in the Church, the nature of the Eucharist, and the role of Mary, showcasing the potential for substantial theological convergence.

Beyond doctrinal discussions, ecumenical dialogues frequently engage in collaborative efforts on social and ethical issues. This cooperation underscores a shared commitment to addressing contemporary challenges such as poverty, injustice, and the defense of human dignity. By working together, Christian denominations witness to a united front that transcends confessional boundaries, reflecting a common mission rooted in the Gospel.

Furthermore, the dialogue with other Christian denominations is not exclusively an intellectual pursuit; it is animated by a spirit of charity and mutual respect. The relational aspect of these dialogues is crucial, as it fosters a sense of fraternity and shared purpose. Personal relationships among theologians, clergy, and laypeople from different denominations often serve as the groundwork for deeper theological exchanges.

Despite the progress made, significant challenges remain. Issues such as the ordination of women, differing views on moral teachings, and varying liturgical practices continue to pose hurdles to full communion. However, the persistence of these dialogues testifies to a commitment to seeking unity that respects diversity. It is an ongoing journey marked by both setbacks and breakthroughs.

Ultimately, the dialogue with other Christian denominations reflects a commitment to the visible unity of the Body of Christ, grounded in a shared faith in Jesus Christ and a common baptism. It is a testament to the enduring relevance of Sacred Tradition as both a source and a sign of this unity. In this endeavor, the Church endeavors not merely to preserve Tradition but to engage it actively, discerning and articulating its truths in ways that resonate across Christian communities.

As the landscape of Christian denominations continues to evolve, the pursuit of unity through dialogue remains a vital aspect of the Church's mission. By engaging deeply with other Christian traditions, the Catholic Church seeks not only to understand and be understood but also to witness to the reconciling power of the Gospel. In the words of Christ, "that they may all be one" (John 17:21) continues to inspire and guide these efforts, affirming the hope that, through the grace of God, divided Christian communities might one day celebrate their unity in faith, hope, and love.

Role of Tradition in Interfaith Relations

Tradition, in its broadest sense, serves as a guiding beacon amidst the labyrinthine journey of interfaith relations. In considering this manifold role, one must first acknowledge that Tradition acts not merely as a static repository of truths but as a dynamic and living transmission of faith through the ages. The functionality of Tradition becomes all the more critical when juxtaposed with the complex arena of interfaith dialogue. By grounding conversations in centuries of theological reflection, Tradition provides a bridge that can span vast doctrinal divides.

The Roman Catholic Church, with its rich tapestry of Tradition, can offer a nuanced platform for interfaith encounters. In this discourse, Tradition is more than historical background; it is an active agent shaping and aiding understanding between diverse faith communities. Consider, for instance, the role of ecumenical councils and papal decrees. These formalized decisions and theological elucidations act as cornerstones upon which the Church builds its stance in interfaith dialogue. They present distilled wisdom that has been scrutinized and validated over time, providing a reliable foundation for discussions on faith, morality, and spiritual practices.

Further accentuating Tradition's role in interfaith relations is its ability to encapsulate the immutable principles of divine revelation. The Catechism of the Catholic Church points to Tradition as "a living transmission, accomplished in the Holy Spirit," allowing it to perpetuate teachings that are both ancient and ever-renewing. This enables Tradition to act as a unifying factor, offering a scriptural continuity that various religious traditions can engage with. For instance, the theological concept of the Logos, which corresponds to the Word of God, finds echoes in multiple religious philosophies, including Judaism and Islam. This shared conceptual ground opens avenues of mutual respect and understanding, thereby fostering a more profound and empathetic interfaith dialogue.

One cannot overlook the pragmatic applications of Tradition in this context. Liturgical practices, sacramental theology, and the writings of

Church Fathers offer rich material for comparative theology. These elements serve as valuable touchstones for illustrating how different faith traditions approach God, worship, and community life. For example, the emphasis on communal worship within Catholic Tradition finds parallel expressions in other faiths, such as Friday prayers in Islam or the Sabbath in Judaism. By situating these practices within the larger framework of human's search for divine communion, Tradition aids in identifying common values and rituals, fostering unity in diversity.

Moreover, the pedagogical role of Tradition cannot be overstated. In interfaith settings, the shared understanding of theological constructs and sacred histories provides a common vocabulary, minimizing potential misunderstandings and misinterpretations. This educational function of Tradition, therefore, equips those engaged in interfaith dialogue with the intellectual tools necessary for sincere and effective communication. Seminary programs and theological faculties often utilize comparative studies that emphasize Tradition to prepare clergy and scholars for interfaith engagements. By fostering a deep understanding of one's own religious heritage, as well as that of others, these academic settings become fertile grounds for nurturing interfaith respect and collaboration.

A historical perspective further enriches this dialogue. Consider how the early Church, through Apostolic Tradition, negotiated its identity amidst a plurality of religious philosophies in the Roman Empire. Figures such as Justin Martyr and Clement of Alexandria engaged with Hellenistic thought, thereby setting a precedent for respectful and enriching interfaith discussions. These early interactions illustrate how a robust engagement with diverse religious traditions can lead to a more profound understanding of one's own faith. This historical precedent serves as a beacon for contemporary interfaith dialogues, encouraging openness, respect, and intellectual engagement.

Modern developments, particularly those spurred by the Second Vatican Council, underscore the evolving role of Tradition in interfaith relations. Vatican II's declaration "Nostra Aetate" stands as a pivotal document that reoriented the Church's approach to non-Christian religions. By emphasizing shared human dignity and the search for existential truths, the document draws upon the wealth of Tradition to advocate for mutual respect and understanding. This modern embodiment of Tradition offers a blueprint for contemporary interfaith efforts, encouraging dialogues that are not only respectful but also theologically enriching.

Theologically speaking, the role of Tradition extends beyond mere dialogue to a transformative encounter. Engaging with other faiths through the lens of Tradition offers a unique opportunity for Catholics to witness to the Gospel. This witness is not a proselytizing effort but rather an invitation to a lived experience of divine love and truth. The sacramentality of Tradition, as seen in the life of the Church, embodies this witness, inviting others to encounter God through the richness of Catholic faith practices, doctrines, and communal life. By doing so, Tradition becomes a living testament to the ever-present reality of divine revelation, inviting all of humanity into a closer relationship with the Creator.

In conclusion, Tradition's role in interfaith relations is multifaceted and profoundly impactful. It provides a stable yet dynamic framework for engaging with other faith traditions, fostering mutual understanding, respect, and shared theological reflection. Through its historical depth, pedagogical applications, and theological richness, Tradition acts as a guiding light for those navigating the complex terrain of interfaith dialogue. By embracing this role, the Church can continue to extend a hand of friendship to other faith communities, promoting peace, understanding, and a shared search for divine truth.

Chapter 11: Theological Tensions and Resolutions

The collaboration and occasional friction between theologians like Yves Congar and Hans Küng exemplify the dynamic discourse within Roman Catholic theology, highlighting the challenges in balancing doctrinal integrity with modern interpretations. Their profound yet differing views constructed a landscape where theological tensions not only surfaced but also sought resolution through critical dialogue and ecclesiastical guidance. Congar's focus on tradition and its organic development contrasted sharply with Küng's more critical stance toward ecclesiastical authority, creating a fertile ground for debate and comparative analysis. These tensions, however, were not mere points of contention but contributed significantly to enriching contemporary theology. By navigating these complex theological waters, the Church both reaffirmed its core beliefs and adapted to the evolving understanding of its sacred traditions, illustrating an ongoing process of discernment and reconciliation.

Congar vs. Küng: Comparative Analysis

The contrasting theological perspectives of Yves Congar and Hans Küng provide a compelling window into the complexities and debates that pervade contemporary Catholic theology, especially in the realm of Sacred Tradition. Both theologians have significantly influenced the understanding of tradition, yet their approaches reflect markedly different paradigms.

Yves Congar, a Dominican priest, is often revered for his foundational contributions to the concept of ecclesiology and his robust defense of tradition as a dynamic and living reality. He viewed tradition not as an unchanging relic of the past but as something evolving through the life of the Church. Congar emphasized the role of the Holy Spirit in guiding the Church and illuminating the deposit of faith continually. This perspective allowed him to argue that tradition and progression are not mutually exclusive but are seamlessly intertwined in the continuity of the Church's life.

In contrast, Hans Küng, a Swiss theologian, brought a more critical and often contentious lens to the concept of tradition. Küng's approach was marked by a drive for reform and a deep concern for what he saw as excessive institutionalism within the Church. His critique of infallibility and his open questioning of established dogmas placed him at odds with the Vatican, leading to both criticism and admiration within the theological community. For Küng, tradition should be subjected to rigorous scrutiny and must be reinterpreted in light of contemporary understanding and sensibilities.

Theological tension between Congar and Küng centers on their differing views on authority and change within the Church. Congar's more measured, organic approach holds that the Church's magisterium, guided by the Holy Spirit, protects and transmits tradition authentically. This denotes tradition as a conduit through which the faith is dynamically lived out, with a recognition of the need for development while respecting the fundamental truths handed down through the ages.

By contrast, Küng championed a democratization of theology, advocating for broader participation in the reformulation of doctrine. He sought to demystify the supposed infallibility of the magisterium, arguing instead for a historical-critical method that treats Church teachings as historically conditioned and therefore subject to reform. His vision of tradition is one that is more fluid and provisional, emphasizing the need for constant revision in dialogue with modern thought and scientific advances.

These competing visions came to a head most noticeably during the reforms of the Second Vatican Council. Congar was a seminal voice in the Council, helping to shape key documents that balanced tradition with aggiornamento, or renewal. Notably, his influence is evident in "Dei Verbum," which articulates the relationship between Scripture and tradition, and in "Lumen Gentium," which speaks to the nature of the Church as a sacramental sign of communion with God. Congar's ability to navigate the tension between the need for continuity and the requirement for change exemplified his balanced yet progressive approach.

Küng's impact on Vatican II was more controversial and complex. While his early works, such as "The Church," were influential, his later positions, particularly criticisms of papal authority, marginalized him from the official proceedings. Nonetheless, his presence loomed large, and his work has perpetuated a critical dialogue within the Church regarding the nature of tradition and the scope of reform.

The comparison between Congar and Küng also highlights differing methodologies in theological inquiry. Congar's method was deeply rooted in the patristic tradition and the historical development of doctrine. He saw value in the lived experience of the Church and perceived the development of doctrine as a reflection of the Church's journey through history. Congar's method is fundamentally historical and theological, integrating a sense of the traditional with contemporary questions.

In contrast, Küng adopted a more interdisciplinary approach, drawing on historical-critical methods, philosophy, and even modern science to challenge traditional views. For Küng, the study of tradition was not just a theological endeavor but an engagement with the broader intellectual currents of the time. His work often crossed into the realms of sociology and modern thought, seeking to make theology relevant to the pressing issues of contemporary society.

Ultimately, the contributions of Congar and Küng represent two poles in the dialogue about tradition within Catholicism: one advocating for a dynamic continuity guided by the Holy Spirit, and the other for a critical and revisionist reappraisal conditioned by modern knowledge and sensibilities. These schools of thought continue to shape contemporary theological discourse, reflecting an ongoing tension about how the Church can remain faithful to its heritage while being responsive to the needs of the present and future.

This tension is not merely academic but has profound implications for ecclesial life and practice. It influences how doctrines are taught, how liturgy is practiced, and how the Church engages with the world. The differing approaches of Congar and Küng provide a framework for understanding the ongoing conversation in the Church about the nature of authority, the role of tradition, and the possibility of change.

The legacies of both theologians underscore the richness and diversity within Catholic thought. Congar's emphasis on the richness of tradition as a living reality juxtaposed with Küng's relentless call for reform and reconsideration provides a fertile ground for reflection and discussion. Their comparative analysis reveals the multilayered and at times contentious nature of theological development within the Church.

The dialogues between the schools of thought represented by Congar and Küng continue to resonate today. The balance between tradition and change can be seen in contemporary debates about liturgical practices, ethical issues, and doctrinal teachings. As the Church navigates the complexities of the modern world, the insights from Congar and Küng offer valuable perspectives on how to remain faithful to the core of Christian belief while dialoguing with contemporary culture.

In conclusion, the study of these two theologians sheds light on the critical and constructive elements of theological discourse within the Catholic tradition. By understanding their contributions and tensions, theologians, scholars, and believers can gain deeper insights into how to approach the ongoing task of interpreting and living out the faith. The interplay between Congar's depth of historical consciousness and Küng's insistence on renewal remains a vital part of Catholic theology's engagement with its past and its future.

Contributions to Contemporary Theology

The interplay between tradition and contemporary theology is not just a discussion but a vital dialogue that forms the fabric of the Catholic Church's ongoing intellectual and spiritual journey. Modern theologians, especially after the Second Vatican Council, have deepened and diversified the understanding of tradition. Their contributions serve as anchors and bridges, offering both continuity and innovation within a framework that remains faithful to the Church's core teachings.

A primary contribution of contemporary theology lies in the nuanced rearticulation of tradition's dynamic nature. Yves Congar, for example, emphasized the living character of tradition, suggesting that it is not a static deposit of faith but a continuous and organic process. His work reassures us that the Church, while anchored in immutable truths, is not bound to antiquated expressions or forms. This balance between fidelity and adaptability is imperative for a Church situated in an ever-evolving cultural and intellectual landscape.

On the other side of the spectrum, Hans Küng offered a more critical stance. Though controversial, his works challenged the Church to reconsider how tradition is applied and interpreted. By questioning certain dogmatic elements, Küng opened up necessary conversations around the authenticity and applicability of long-held beliefs. These discussions, though at times contentious, have propelled forward deeper investigations into doctrine, encouraging a more profound engagement with sacred texts and ecclesiastical practices.

The contributions of these theologians create space for an enriched ecclesial life where tradition is in constant dialogue with contemporary contexts. They highlight the tension often felt between maintaining orthodoxy and fostering pastoral relevance, urging the Church to be both unchanging in its truths and responsive to the world's needs.

Furthermore, the emphasis on collegiality and the sensus fidei (sense of the faithful) have been instrumental in shaping contemporary Catholic theology. Drawing from the ecclesiological shifts of Vatican II, contemporary theologians integrate the voices of the laity more robustly into theological discourse. This democratization within the theological community helps ensure that the lived experiences of the faithful are taken into account, thereby preventing a solely top-down approach to tradition. Such a participatory model underlines that tradition is the inheritance of the entire Church, not just its hierarchy.

Another significant contribution to contemporary theology has been the expansion of interfaith and ecumenical dialogue. This spirit of openness stems directly from a renewed understanding of tradition as inclusive and dialogical. Theologians have worked tirelessly to emphasize commonalities with other denominations and faith traditions, seeking to heal rifts and build bridges. This dialogue is not merely a theological exercise but a testament to a Church committed to peace, reconciliation, and mutual understanding, enriching the very fabric of tradition itself.

Environmental theology has also found a more pronounced voice in recent years. Rooted in the concept of stewardship from the Genesis narrative, contemporary theologians have expanded this to address modern ecological crises. By situating environmental concerns within the framework of tradition, theologians emphasize the Church's call to safeguard creation, thus reflecting a tradition that speaks to contemporary global challenges.

Moreover, liberation theology, predominantly emerging from Latin America, signifies another dimensional shift. It interprets tradition through the lens of the oppressed, aligning the Church's mission with social justice imperatives. This perspective challenges the Church to be prophetic, extending its tradition of care and advocacy to modern contexts of poverty and injustice, reinforcing the Gospel's call to "bring good news to the poor" (Luke 4:18).

As we navigate these multiple contributions, it becomes evident that contemporary theology doesn't seek to discard tradition but to rejuvenate and mobilize it. The proliferation of theological perspectives enriches the Church's doctrinal patrimony, ensuring it remains a living, breathing testament to divine revelation.

We observe that theological discourse today is marked by a profound commitment to contextually dialoguing with tradition. Various movements within theology, from feminist to queer to postcolonial theologies, offer critical insights into how tradition can be inclusive and reflective of diverse human experiences. These contributions do not dilute tradition; instead, they invite the Church to comprehend the universality of its mission in ever-expanding ways.

The engagement with science and modernity, too, facilitates an enriching dialogue. Theologians like Pierre Teilhard de Chardin paved the way for seeing faith and science not as adversaries but as partners in understanding divine reality. His concept of the Omega Point, while controversial, provides a framework where evolution and eschatology are intertwined, inviting a synthesis of scientific knowledge and traditional eschatological hope.

Finally, contemporary theology's contribution is seen in the realm of pastoral care. The complexities of modern life, ranging from technological advancements to social disintegration, require a theology that is responsive and pastoral. Theologians are called to translate tradition into a language and practice that resonate with today's faithful. This pastoral dimension ensures that tradition remains a source of comfort, guidance, and hope.

In summary, the robust contributions of contemporary theology to tradition demonstrate a Church that is ever ancient and ever new. It highlights a theological enterprise that is faithful yet dynamic, historical yet contemporary, doctrinal yet pastoral. It celebrates a tradition that, enriched by the voices of contemporary theologians, continues to be a living channel of divine grace and truth.

Chapter 12: The Future of Tradition in a Changing World

As we stand at the crossroads of tradition and modernity, the future of Sacred Tradition in a rapidly evolving world presents both formidable challenges and dynamic opportunities. The immutable truths revealed through God's church must be navigated amidst the tides of cultural shifts, technological advancements, and an ever-globalizing society. Scholars and theologians find themselves tasked with discerning how to faithfully maintain and convey these truths without compromise, yet with an ardent awareness of contemporary demands. Envisioning an adaptive yet resoluitive tradition, the Catholic Church must confront questions of relevancy, identity, and cohesion, striving to nurture a living faith that speaks to today's hearts without losing its doctrinal essence. The potential for growth lies in a dialogue that respects the rich heritage of the past while courageously stepping into the unknown future, ensuring that the beacon of tradition continues to illuminate, guide, and inspire in an ever-changing world.

Challenges and Opportunities

The intersection of tradition and modernity presents both formidable challenges and unique opportunities for the Roman Catholic Church. One of the most pressing challenges is the preservation of doctrinal purity in an era characterized by rapid cultural and technological changes. The truths encapsulated within Sacred Tradition were handed down through the centuries, gaining layers of interpretation and understanding. However, these immutable truths now face the pressure of remaining relevant in the face of ever-evolving societal norms.

Among the more profound challenges is the secularization of society, which has led to a diminishing role of religion in public life. Secular philosophies often conflict with Catholic teachings, necessitating a dialogue that can sometimes appear as a contentious battleground. Tradition, which has long served as a bedrock for faith and morals, is under scrutiny by a populace that increasingly values skepticism and relativism. This environment makes it crucial for theologians and scholars to find ways to communicate ancient truths in a manner that resonates with contemporary audiences.

Additionally, internal dissensions within the Church can hinder its ability to present a unified front in the face of external challenges. Differences in theological interpretation, such as those noted between figures like Yves Congar and Hans Küng, must be navigated carefully. These internal debates can either serve as a source of richness, providing multiple avenues for understanding and applying tradition, or they can become points of contention that weaken the Church's cohesion.

On the other hand, these challenges also bring about significant opportunities. The digital age offers unprecedented avenues for evangelization and catechesis. Online platforms can be leveraged to disseminate Church teachings, making the depth and richness of Catholic Tradition accessible to a global audience. Such initiatives can provide a new vitality to the practice of faith, fostering a more engaged and informed Catholic community.

There is also the opportunity for interfaith dialogue to broaden the scope of tradition. Engaging with other Christian denominations and world religions can enrich Catholic theology, lending new perspectives and insights. The Catholic commitment to ecumenism, which gained emphasis during the Second Vatican Council, continues to provide a framework for these interactions. By participating in such dialogues, the Church can both affirm its own traditions and respect the spiritual wealth found in other faith communities.

Moreover, the challenges posed by modernity can inspire a reevaluation and deeper understanding of tradition. Theological inquiry that critically engages with contemporary issues can lead to a more robust articulation of the faith. For instance, the Humanities and Social Sciences offer tools that can complement theological study, enabling scholars to address questions regarding social justice, human dignity, and moral relativism from a solidly Catholic perspective.

The changing world also propels the Church towards greater inclusivity and diversity. As the global Church continues to grow, particularly in regions like Africa, Asia, and Latin America, there is a dynamic opportunity to integrate diverse cultural expressions into the practice and understanding of tradition. This cultural multiplicity not only enriches the Church's liturgy and communal life but also poses questions about how universal truths are understood and lived in various contexts.

Vatican II's call for aggiornamento, or updating, remains pertinent. This renewal doesn't imply a departure from fundamental teachings but encourages a rejuvenation of faith practice. It's a challenge to apply eternal truths in ways that respond to contemporary circumstances without compromising their integrity. These efforts can reinvigorate parish life, influence social teachings, and impact educational frameworks within and outside the Church.

Institutional and structural adaptations are necessary to meet these contemporary challenges effectively. Seminaries, theological faculties, and catechetical programs must all be attuned to the current cultural climate. This might involve incorporating newer methods of pedagogy that respect tradition while engaging with modern academic and social developments. The integration of science and technology, for instance, can provide novel insights that bolster the Church's mission.

The role of the laity offers another significant opportunity in this evolving landscape. Lay Catholics are increasingly taking up leadership roles within the Church, contributing their expertise and passion to various forms of ministry and social action. Bishop and clergy can benefit immensely from the insights and experiences of a well-formed laity. Programs aimed at lay formation can play a pivotal role in this regard, ensuring that the contributions of laypersons align with and enhance the Church's mission.

Finally, the resilience of Catholic Social Teaching presents both a challenge and an opportunity. On one hand, applying these teachings in a world rife with systemic inequalities and environmental crises remains a daunting task. On the other hand, the Church's longstanding commitment to social justice provides a powerful platform for advocacy and action. Addressing issues like poverty, human trafficking, and ecological destruction can demonstrate the timeless relevance of Catholic Tradition in promoting the common good.

In summary, while the changing world presents myriad challenges, it equally offers opportunities for the Church to reaffirm and renew her commitment to Sacred Tradition. Engaging effectively with these dynamics will require wisdom, courage, and a deep reliance on the Holy Spirit. As theologians, scholars, historians, and the faithful navigate these frontiers, they have the collective task of ensuring that the transmission of immutable truths remains both vibrant and relevant.

Prospects for the Evolution of Tradition

As the tides of time relentlessly march forward, the Catholic Church stands as a bastion of immutable truths intertwined with evolving human contexts. Tradition, which has carried the essence of the Church's doctrines, is not a static entity but a living, dynamic process. The prospects for the evolution of tradition invite a thoughtful examination of how sacred teachings might continue to develop and adapt in a rapidly changing world while remaining anchored to their divine origin.

The very essence of tradition lies in its dual nature: it must be both preservative and adaptive. This paradox is at the heart of its evolution. Tradition safeguards the core tenets of the faith, ensuring continuity with the past. Simultaneously, it must respond to new challenges, contexts, and understandings. Indeed, the Church finds itself at the intersection of history and modernity, inviting a complex dance between maintaining doctrinal purity and meeting contemporary pastoral needs.

Modern challenges such as technological advancements, secularization, and globalization compel the Church to reconsider how it communicates and incarnates timeless truths. The digital age, for example, transforms not only the means of evangelization but also the very nature of community and catechesis. Tradition will likely evolve by integrating digital platforms, fostering new ways to engage the faithful while retaining the sacrosanct core of the message.

Furthermore, the ongoing dialogue between faith and reason signifies a profound area for the evolution of tradition. Philosophical and scientific advancements constantly stretch the horizons of human understanding. Thus, Catholic theology, grounded in tradition, is called to engage thoughtfully with contemporary thought systems. Such engagement does not dilute the tradition; rather, it enriches it by offering deeper insights into divine mysteries in light of new knowledge.

Moreover, the process of inculturation highlights another prospect for the evolution of tradition. The Church, in her missionary aspect, must discern how to authentically present the Gospel within various cultural milieus. This process respects the integrity of local traditions while promoting the universality of the faith. It is a delicate balance of respecting diversity and ensuring doctrinal unity—a dynamic interplay that characterizes true tradition.

Ecumenism also shapes the path forward for tradition. In an age where unity among Christian denominations is increasingly emphasized, the evolution of tradition involves a re-engagement with shared beliefs while addressing theological divergences. This pursuit of unity does not abandon foundational truths but seeks common ground, fostering a mutual enrichment among Christian traditions.

It is important to recognize how Vatican II exemplifies such an evolution. The Council marked a significant moment in the Church's history, reflecting Tradition's ability to renew and speak to contemporary humanity. The aggiornamento, or updating, called for by St. John XXIII, illustrates tradition's capacity for reformation without forfeiting its essence. The implementation of vernacular languages in the liturgy, for instance, exemplifies how tradition can transform to facilitate fuller participation of the faithful in the sacred mysteries.

As contemporary society continues to grapple with moral and ethical questions, the Church must articulate her teachings in a manner that speaks compellingly to these issues. The moral doctrines, steeped in tradition, face new scenarios brought about by advances in bioethics, human rights, and social justice. Tradition, therefore, must evolve to address these modern concerns while remaining faithful to its Scriptural and theological heritage.

Furthermore, the Church's magisterium plays a crucial role in this evolutionary process. This teaching authority, led by the Holy Spirit, ensures continuity with apostolic faith while discerning how best to respond to the signs of the times. The magisterium's role in the evolution of tradition is both a safeguard and a progressive force, ensuring that doctrinal development is coherent and consonant with the faith once delivered to the saints.

The involvement of the laity in this evolutionary process also signifies a hopeful prospect. The sensus fidelium, or the sense of the faithful, underscores the importance of the whole Church in discerning and living out tradition. In our democratic age, this ancient concept finds new vigor, emphasizing the laypersons' role in witnessing to and shaping the faith within diverse contexts and challenges.

In conclusion, the evolution of tradition is not a sign of compromise but an invitation to deeper fidelity. As the Church moves forward, she does so with the surety that Christ, the same yesterday, today, and forever, guides her. The prospects for the evolution of tradition promise a future where ancient truths resound with fresh clarity, speaking anew to every generation in the unending journey towards the fullness of truth.

Conclusion

The exploration of Catholic theology, as navigated through the continuum of Sacred Tradition, reveals a remarkable narrative of doctrinal development, communal faith, and theological resilience. From the early apostolic era to the post-Vatican II landscape, the Church's journey to elucidate and embody the truths entrusted to her has been both complex and rich with meaning. These truths, though immutable and eternal, find their expression ever new in varying epochs and cultures, thereby engaging humanity in an ongoing dialogue with the divine.

Throughout this examination, it has become evident that Sacred Tradition acts as a vital lifeline, connecting the faithful across generations. While Scripture undeniably plays an essential role, the interplay between Scripture and Tradition, particularly highlighted in Chapter 4, underscores their coexistence and mutual reinforcement. As the Apostolic Fathers and the early ecumenical councils laid foundational understandings, so too did subsequent scholars, and Church leaders contribute through councils, debates, and practices.

The theological insights of influential figures such as Yves Congar and Hans Küng, discussed in Chapters 2 and 3, respectively, illustrate the dynamic nature of Tradition. Congar's focus on ecclesiology and Küng's often controversial critiques provide a spectrum of interpretation and application, demonstrating that wrestling with Tradition is not a genteel exercise but a vigorous endeavor. The contrasts in their approaches also underscore a broader tension within the Church, detailed further in Chapter 11, wherein dialogue and dissent coexist, ultimately contributing to a richer, more tempered faith.

Medieval contributions, especially from the Scholastics, enriched Tradition through their synthesis of reason and faith. By integrating philosophical rigor with theological inquiry, these scholars laid groundwork that informed later reforms and counter-reformations, as detailed in Chapters 6 and 7. The Protestant Reformation posed significant challenges to Catholic Tradition, calling for a deep introspection within the Church and culminating in the Council of Trent's robust affirmation of the same.

The modern epoch heralded by Enlightenment and further accelerated by contemporary thought, as examined in Chapter 8, has been particularly transformative. The Second Vatican Council represents a pivotal moment where Tradition saw both continuity and adaptation. This era provides a nuanced view where past and present converge, aiming to remain faithful to the core while speaking authentically to the contemporary soul.

Central to Tradition's efficacy is the role of the Magisterium, the teaching authority of the Church, discussed thoroughly in Chapter 9. Its guidance ensures that the interpretation and application of faith remain coherent and consistent with apostolic teaching. Liturgical practices and sacraments, timeless in their essence, continually find renewed significance through the lens of Tradition, illustrating how the sacred continues to be relevant in an ever-changing world.

The ecumenical dialogues surveyed in Chapter 10 remind us that Tradition's richness is not merely for internal edification but also serves as a bridge to other Christian denominations and faith traditions. In engaging with others, the Church exercises a profound aspect of Tradition: to be a living testimony of unity and love as Christ prayed for all his followers.

Theological tensions, such as those between Congar and Küng, are not mere academic quarrels but reflect the robust nature of the theological enterprise within Catholicism. Chapter 11's comparative analysis highlights how such tensions drive deeper inquiry and more comprehensive resolutions, contributing to a dynamic and living Tradition capable of facing contemporary challenges.

Looking forward, Chapter 12 invites reflection on Tradition's place in an increasingly globalized and pluralistic society. The Church's commitment to preserving doctrine while engaging with modernity offers both challenges and exciting opportunities. As digital advancements and cultural shifts redefine how communities operate, Tradition remains a steadfast compass, guiding the faithful through uncertain terrains with the promise of perennial truths.

In sum, the unfolding narrative of Sacred Tradition within Catholic theology is one of both continuity and creativity. It is not a static adherence to past formulas but a vibrant engagement with the living Word, ever ancient and ever new. This theological and historical journey reveals how the Church, through the cohesion of Scripture and Tradition, stands as a testament to humanity's ongoing quest to fathom and live out the eternal truths revealed by God. The struggle to grasp these truths is a testament to both the mystery of the divine and the depth of human yearning.

The study of Sacred Tradition, far from being an arcane endeavor, speaks to the heart of what it means to belong to the Church. It calls theologians, scholars, Roman Catholics, historians, and philosophers alike to delve deeper, to question and to contemplate with humility and fervor. This journey, intricate and expansive, continues to shape the fabric of faith communities, ensuring that the Church remains ever faithful, ever relevant, and ever a beacon of divine truth in the world.

Appendix A: Appendix

This appendix aims to provide supplementary materials and insights to support the main text of the book. Herein, we've gathered various resources, additional readings, and important references that contribute to a fuller understanding of Catholic theology, Sacred Tradition, and the development of Sacred Scripture.

Primary Sources

For a deeper dive into the foundational texts of Catholic tradition, we recommend exploring the following primary sources:

- *Patrologia Latina* edited by Jacques-Paul Migne, an extensive collection of writings by the Latin Church Fathers.
- *Scripturae Sacrae*, including collections of Biblical canon and Apocryphal texts.
- *Decrees of the Ecumenical Councils* by Norman P. Tanner, encapsulating the key council documents from Nicaea to Vatican II.

Scholarly Works

The following scholars have done extensive work on the subjects covered in this book, providing invaluable commentary and analytical insights:

- Yves Congar: Particularly his works *Tradition and Traditions* and *The Meaning of Tradition*.
- Hans Küng: Notably, *The Church* and *The Catholic Church: A Short History*.
- Jaroslav Pelikan: Especially his multi-volume series, *The Christian Tradition: A History of the Development of Doctrine*.

Contemporary Studies

Recent studies have continued to add layers of interpretation and scholarship to our understanding of Tradition and Scripture. Works such as:

- *Catholic Theology: An Introduction* by Frederick C. Bauerschmidt and James J. Buckley.
- *Tradition and the Church* by John E. Thiel.
- *The Church and the Modern Era (1846-2005): Pius IX, World Wars, and Vatican II* by David M. Wagner.

Key Ecclesiastical Documents

The following documents from the Magisterium are essential for anyone looking to understand the official stance of the Church on matters of Tradition and Scripture:

- *Dei Verbum* (Dogmatic Constitution on Divine Revelation) from the Second Vatican Council.
- *Lamentabili Sane,* Holy See's syllabus of errors condemning modernist interpretations.
- *Catechism of the Catholic Church*, providing comprehensive insight into Church doctrines and teachings.

Prominent Figures

For quick reference, the following figures make frequent appearances throughout this work and are pivotal to understanding the development and expression of Catholic theology:

- **St. Augustine** - Influential early theologian whose works on grace, free will, and the Church continue to resonate.
- **St. Thomas Aquinas** - His synthesis of Aristotelian philosophy with Christian doctrine remains a cornerstone of Catholic theology.
- **John Henry Newman** - His theory of the development of doctrine has shaped modern theological approaches.

This appendix serves as a roadmap for further exploration into the themes discussed in the book. Leveraging these resources will enrich one's understanding and provide greater context to the interplay of Tradition, Scripture, and theology across the ages.

Glossary of Theological Terms

This glossary aims to provide clear and concise definitions of key theological terms relevant to Roman Catholic theology and its traditions. The listed terms are instrumental in understanding how Catholic theology and Sacred Scripture have developed through Sacred Tradition over the centuries.

Apophatic Theology

A form of theological thinking and religious practice which attempts to approach the divine by negation, to speak only in terms of what may not be said about the perfect goodness that is God.

Apostolicity

The characteristic of the Church being rooted in the apostles through an unbroken historical and spiritual continuity, emphasizing adherence to the apostles' teachings and traditions.

Canon

The official list of books recognized by a religious community as divinely inspired and constituting their sacred scriptures. In Catholicism, this refers to the books of the Old and New Testaments accepted by the Church.

Dogma

Beliefs or doctrines that are proclaimed as undoubtedly true by a religious authority. In Catholic theology, these are truths revealed by God and necessitate the assent of faith by all Catholics.

Ecumenism

The initiative aimed at promoting unity among different Christian denominations and traditions through dialogue and cooperation.

Epistemology

The branch of philosophy that studies the nature, origin, and limits of human knowledge. In theology, it explores the foundation of theological knowledge and belief.

Heresy

A belief or opinion that deviates from the established doctrines of a religious organization, particularly those that contradict Catholic dogma.

Magisterium

The teaching authority of the Roman Catholic Church, vested in the Pope and the bishops, whose role is to interpret and preserve the truths of faith contained in Sacred Scripture and Sacred Tradition.

Marian Doctrine

Teachings of the Catholic Church related to Mary, the mother of Jesus, encompassing her divine motherhood, perpetual virginity, Immaculate Conception, and Assumption.

Orthodoxy

Adherence to accepted and traditional teachings of the faith. In a broader context, it refers to beliefs conforming to the authorized doctrines and creeds of the Church.

Patristics

The study of the writings and teachings of the early Church Fathers, whose works were pivotal in the development of Christian doctrine and theology.

Sacred Tradition

The living transmission of the message of the Gospel in the Church. It encompasses the teachings, life, and worship of the Church as handed down through the ages from the apostles.

Scholasticism

A medieval school of philosophy and theology that sought to reconcile faith with reason through systematic argumentation and critical analysis. A prominent proponent was Thomas Aquinas.

Soteriology

The study of religious doctrines concerning salvation. In Christianity, it deals with how Christ's life, death, and resurrection bring about human redemption.

Tradition

The process and content of transmission of beliefs, doctrines, practices, rituals, and scriptures from one generation to the next. In Catholicism, it is seen as a fundamental source of divine revelation alongside Sacred Scripture.

Transubstantiation

The doctrine that during the Eucharist, the substance of bread and wine is converted into the actual body and blood of Christ, while the appearances of bread and wine remain.

This glossary serves as a foundational reference for understanding the essential terms and concepts that shape Catholic theology and its intricate relationship with Sacred Tradition.

Biographical Notes on Key Figures

In the rich tapestry of Catholic theology and historical development, numerous figures have played critical roles in shaping the understanding and preservation of Sacred Tradition. Each of these individuals brought unique perspectives, challenges, and contributions that collectively underpin the Roman Catholic Church's theological framework.

St. Augustine of Hippo (354-430 A.D.): A towering intellect in early Christian theology, Augustine's influence spans across doctrines including original sin, grace, and the nature of the Church. He fused Platonic philosophy with Christian teachings, profoundly affecting the theological narrative. His extensive writings, such as "*The Confessions*" and "*City of God*," remain foundational to theological studies and ecclesiastical teachings.

St. Thomas Aquinas (1225-1274 A.D.): A seminal medieval theologian, Aquinas attempted to reconcile Aristotelian philosophy with Christian doctrine. His magnum opus, "*Summa Theologica*," offers a comprehensive synthesis of theology and philosophy. His work on natural law, virtue ethics, and the nature of God has had a lasting impact, making him a central figure in Scholasticism and a Doctor of the Church.

St. Anselm of Canterbury (1033-1109 A.D.): Known for his ontological argument for God's existence and his theological method of "faith seeking understanding," Anselm laid the groundwork for later scholastic endeavors. His treatises, particularly "*Proslogion*," are pivotal in bridging the gap between faith and reason.

St. Gregory the Great (540-604 A.D.): As Pope, Gregory I was instrumental in the early medieval Church's consolidation and doctrinal reinforcement. His theological contributions, pastoral care reforms, and liturgical innovations, including the Gregorian Chant, have left an indelible mark on Church practices and traditions.

St. John of Damascus (676-749 A.D.): A key figure in the defense against iconoclasm, John's work provided strong theological arguments supporting the veneration of icons. His "*Fount of Knowledge*" represents one of the first comprehensive summaries of Christian dogma, blending Greek philosophical concepts with theological insights.

Yves Congar (1904-1995 A.D.): A 20th-century Dominican theologian, Congar's extensive work on ecclesiology and Tradition reshaped contemporary Catholic thought. His writings on the Holy Spirit, the nature of the Church, and ecumenism, particularly in "*I Believe in the Holy Spirit,*" have had a profound influence on Vatican II reforms.

Hans Küng (1928-2021 A.D.): An influential but controversial theologian, Küng's perspectives often challenged traditional Catholic teachings from within. His works, such as "*On Being a Christian,*" aimed at bridging modern secular thought and fundamental Christian beliefs, contributing significantly to contemporary theological discourse.

St. Irenaeus of Lyons (130-202 A.D.): An early Church Father, Irenaeus is best known for his work "*Against Heresies,*" which defended Christian orthodoxy against Gnosticism. His emphasis on apostolic tradition as a means of preserving true doctrine has been crucial in shaping the Church's understanding of Sacred Tradition.

Origen of Alexandria (184-253 A.D.): A pioneering theologian and biblical scholar, Origen's exegetical and theological innovations were both groundbreaking and contentious. His works, such as "*De Principiis,*" introduced allegorical interpretation of Scripture and set a framework for subsequent theological reflection.

St. Justin Martyr (100-165 A.D.): One of the earliest Christian apologists, Justin Martyr's writings formed a crucial bridge between Hellenistic philosophy and nascent Christian theology. His "*First Apology*" advocated for the rational nature of Christian faith, addressing pagan criticisms and influencing early doctrinal formulations.

St. Athanasius of Alexandria (296-373 A.D.): A staunch defender against Arianism, Athanasius's theological and ecclesiastical efforts were pivotal in affirming the doctrine of the Trinity. His "*On the Incarnation*" remains a key theological text expounding the nature of Christ and the significance of His incarnation.

St. Teresa of Ávila (1515-1582 A.D.): A mystic and reformer, Teresa's contributions to Carmelite reforms and her mystical writings, such as "*The Interior Castle,*" provide profound insights into spiritual life and the contemplative tradition within the Church.

St. Francis of Assisi (1181-1226 A.D.): Founder of the Franciscan Order, Francis's emphasis on poverty, humility, and love for all creation reshaped Catholic devotional life and practice. His "*Canticle of the Sun*" reflects his deep engagement with the natural world and commitment to living out the Gospels.

Blessed John Henry Newman (1801-1890 A.D.): A convert from Anglicanism, Newman's theological work on the development of Christian doctrine influenced both Protestant and Catholic thought. His "*Essay on the Development of Christian Doctrine*" articulated how Catholic teachings evolved in continuity with apostolic tradition.

St. Ignatius of Loyola (1491-1556 A.D.): Founder of the Society of Jesus (Jesuits), Ignatius's spiritual exercises and emphasis on education and missionary work played a critical role in the Catholic Reformation. His "*Spiritual Exercises*" remain a significant resource for discerning God's will and deepening spiritual life.

St. Basil the Great (329-379 A.D.): An influential theologian and monastic reformer, Basil's contributions to Trinitarian theology and his monastic rules shaped Eastern Orthodox and Catholic monastic practices. His writings on the Holy Spirit elucidate the co-equality of the Trinity.

St. Benedict of Nursia (480-547 A.D.): Father of Western monasticism, Benedict's "*Rule*" established a balanced path of monastic life, emphasizing ora et labora (prayer and work). His principles have guided monastic communities and influenced Western spiritual thought for centuries.

These biographical notes serve as a testament to the enduring legacy of these key figures whose theological advancements and lived faith continue to resonate within the Church. Through their writings, reforms, and unwavering commitment to the pursuit of truth, each has indelibly shaped the trajectory of Catholic Tradition, guiding both scholars and the faithful in the understanding of divine revelation

Selected Bibliography

The "Selected Bibliography" is an essential component for anyone engaged in the deep exploration of Catholic theology and its intricate relationship with Sacred Tradition and Scripture. This section aims to provide scholars and theologians with a curated list of impactful works that have significantly contributed to the understanding of these profound areas. By providing access to a comprehensive array of texts, readers can further delve into the complexities and nuances that have shaped theological discourse over the centuries.

One of the foundational texts to consider is "On the Development of Christian Doctrine" by John Henry Newman. This seminal work explores how doctrine evolves over time while remaining true to its original divine revelation. Newman's insights lay a crucial groundwork for understanding the dynamic yet consistent nature of Catholic tradition.

Yves Congar's "Tradition and Traditions" is another indispensable resource, illuminating his perspectives on how Sacred Tradition functions within the Church. Congar meticulously examines the role of tradition in maintaining doctrinal continuity and its interaction with the lived experiences of the faithful. His exhaustive scholarship offers invaluable insights into the organic development of tradition.

For those interested in a critical approach, Hans Küng's "The Church" is a key text. Although Küng's positions often sparked controversy, his rigorous analysis challenges assumptions and encourages deeper examination of how tradition is interpreted and applied. His work is essential for understanding diverse perspectives within Catholic theology.

The writings of the Church Fathers, including Augustine's "Confessions" and "City of God" as well as Athanasius's "On the Incarnation," provide foundational perspectives on early Christian doctrine and the role of tradition in the nascent Church. These texts offer glimpses into the theological and philosophical milieu that shaped early Christian thought.

Thomas Aquinas's "Summa Theologica" stands as a monumental achievement in the history of theological thought. Aquinas's synthesis of Aristotelian philosophy with Christian doctrine offers a profound and systematic exploration of many theological issues, making it a cornerstone for anyone delving into medieval perspectives on tradition.

For a deeper understanding of the Reformation and its impact on tradition, Martin Luther's "95 Theses" and John Calvin's "Institutes of the Christian Religion" are critical readings. These works provide context on Protestant challenges to Catholic tradition and illuminate the theological rifts that necessitated responses from within the Catholic Church, such as the decrees from the Council of Trent.

Moving into more contemporary examinations, "Vatican II: Reforming Liturgy" by Massimo Faggioli provides a scholarly analysis of the Second Vatican Council's impacts on liturgical practices and their broader implications for Sacred Tradition. His work sheds light on how modernity influences and reshapes tradition within the Catholic context.

Additional modern resources include Pope Benedict XVI's "Jesus of Nazareth" series, which offers a profound theological reflection on the person and work of Jesus, merging historical critical methods with faith-based approaches. This series provides an integrated view of Scripture and tradition that is both scholarly and devotional.

For a more comprehensive historical overview, Warren H. Carroll's multi-volume work "A History of Christendom" offers an exhaustive narrative of the Church's history, richly detailing how tradition has evolved and been understood through various epochs. Carroll's work helps situate theological developments within broader historical and cultural contexts.

Another invaluable resource is "The Sources of Catholic Dogma" (Denzinger), a compilation of significant creeds, definitions, and declarations of the councils and popes. This collection is essential for anyone looking to understand the authoritative statements that guide Catholic doctrine.

The works of contemporary theologians such as Joseph Ratzinger (Pope Benedict XVI) and Henri de Lubac provide further insights into the continuities and changes within Catholic tradition. Ratzinger's "Introduction to Christianity" and de Lubac's "Catholicism" offer deep and reflective analyses, situating traditional doctrines within the context of modern challenges and understandings.

Lumen Gentium, one of the principal documents from the Second Vatican Council, offers crucial insights into the Church's understanding of itself, particularly in relation to tradition and scripture. This text is indispensable for understanding the ecclesiological underpinnings that guide the Catholic Church's approach to tradition.

For scholars interested in the intersection of tradition and ecumenism, "Unitatis Redintegratio" (Decree on Ecumenism from Vatican II) provides a theological foundation for dialogue with other Christian denominations, emphasizing the role of tradition in fostering unity and understanding.

Lastly, for a philosophical perspective, Alasdair MacIntyre's "After Virtue" is highly recommended. While not exclusively theological, MacIntyre's examination of moral philosophy through the lens of tradition offers valuable insights that resonate deeply with theological concerns about the continuity and development of ethical teachings within Catholicism.

This carefully selected bibliography is designed to equip theologians, scholars, historians, and philosophers with the critical resources necessary to navigate and understand the complex tapestry of Catholic theology, Sacred Tradition, and Scripture. Through the engagement with these texts, readers will gain a richer, more nuanced appreciation of the dynamic interplay between historical contexts and divine revelation.

As we continue to wrestle with the immutable truths of our faith in a constantly changing world, this collection of works will serve as a vital reference point, grounding scholarly inquiry and theological reflection in the rich soil of tradition and authoritative teaching.